When sharks Attack with kindness

Andrews McMeel Publishing
a division of Andrews McMeel Universal
1130 Walnut Street, Kansas City, Missouri 64106

www.andrewsmcmeel.com

21 22 23 24 25 SDB 10 9 8 7 6 5 4 3 2

ISBN: 978-1-5248-6481-1
Library of Congress Control Number: 2020945453

Editor: Lucas Wetzel
Art Director: Spencer Williams
Production Editor: Jasmine Lim
Production Manager: Tamara Haus

ATTENTION: SCHOOLS AND BUSINESSES

Andrews McMeel books are available at quantity discounts with bulk purchase for educational, business, or sales promotional use. For information, please e-mail the Andrews McMeel Publishing Special Sales Department: specialsales@amuniversal.com.

When sharks Attack with kindness

wawa
wiwa

Andrés J. Colmenares

Andrews McMeel
PUBLISHING®

- To my
  wife, the head
  of this family. Our
  children, Adrián and Oli-
  via, you are the legs. My
  dad, mom, and brother, Oscar,
  the arms (yes, this family has
  three arms). My readers, you are
  the feet who move everything for-
  ward. And me, I'm the coffee. I just
  make everyone feel anxious. Thanks.

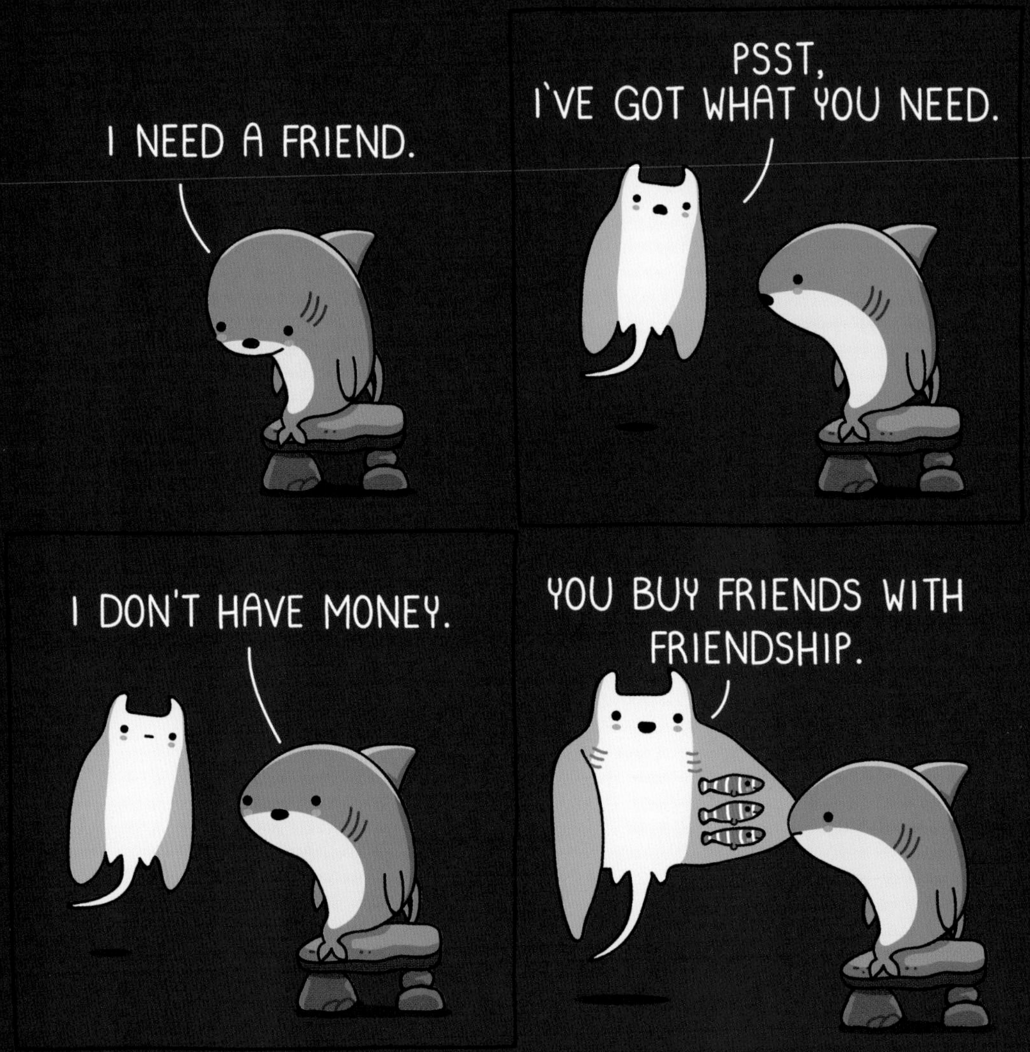
I NEED A FRIEND.
PSST,
I'VE GOT WHAT YOU NEED.
I DON'T HAVE MONEY.
YOU BUY FRIENDS WITH FRIENDSHIP.

Friendships can be really hard to find and hold on to. They can come in different shapes and sizes, and some people can go through life having just one when it's the real deal.
This is a book about kindness, relationships, and love, and since these are such deep subjects, I've made it underwater.

Marine creatures in this book

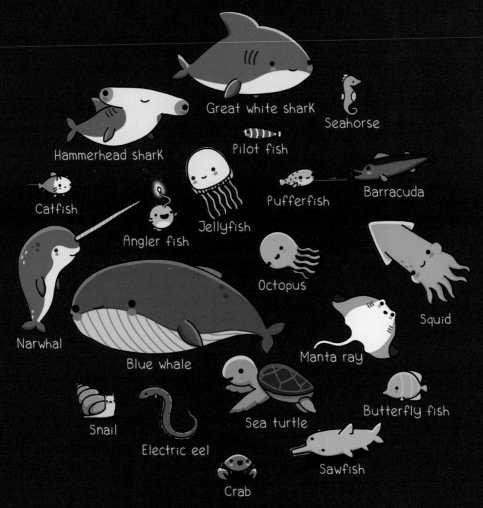

Great white shark

Seahorse

Hammerhead shark

Pilot fish

Catfish

Angler fish

Jellyfish

Pufferfish

Barracuda

Octopus

Squid

Narwhal

Blue whale

Manta ray

Snail

Sea turtle

Butterfly fish

Electric eel

Sawfish

Crab

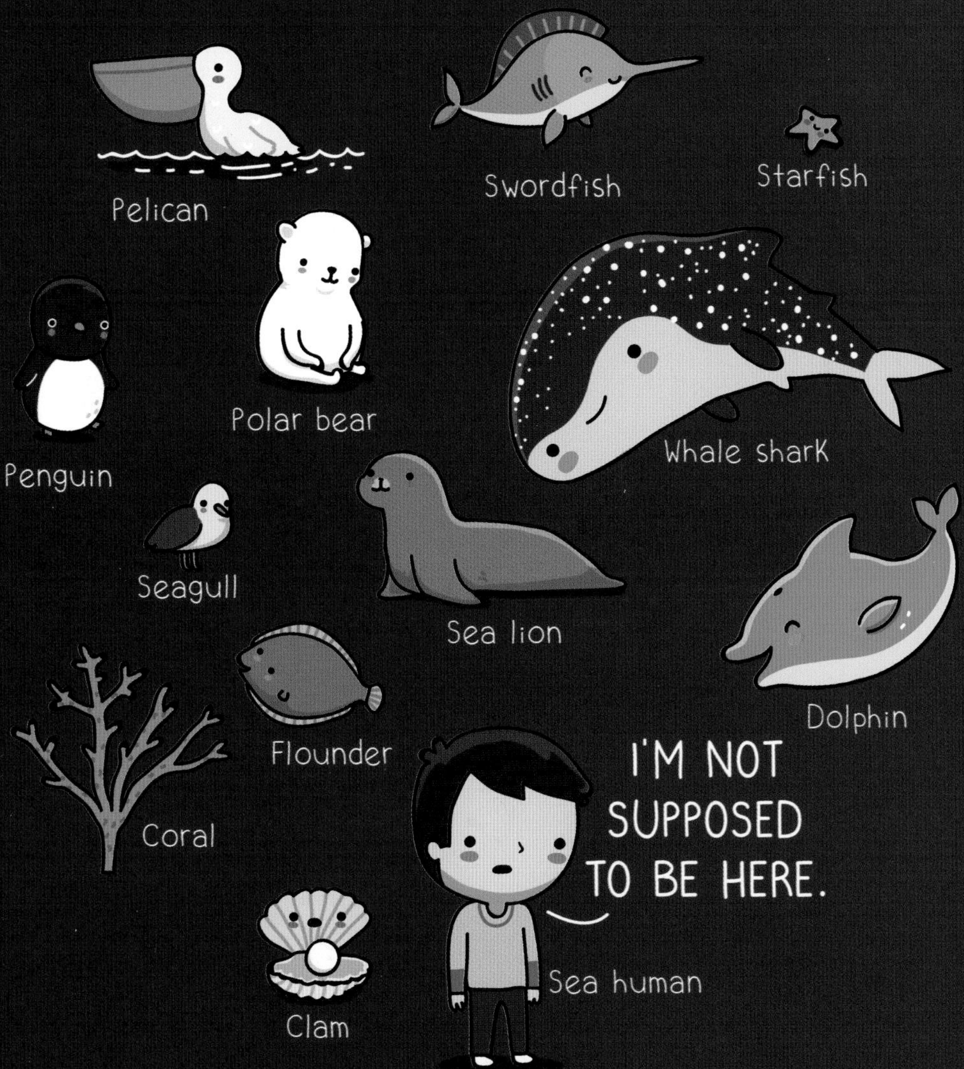
Pelican
Swordfish
Starfish
Polar bear
Penguin
Whale shark
Seagull
Sea lion
Dolphin
Coral
Flounder
I'M NOT SUPPOSED TO BE HERE.
Clam
Sea human

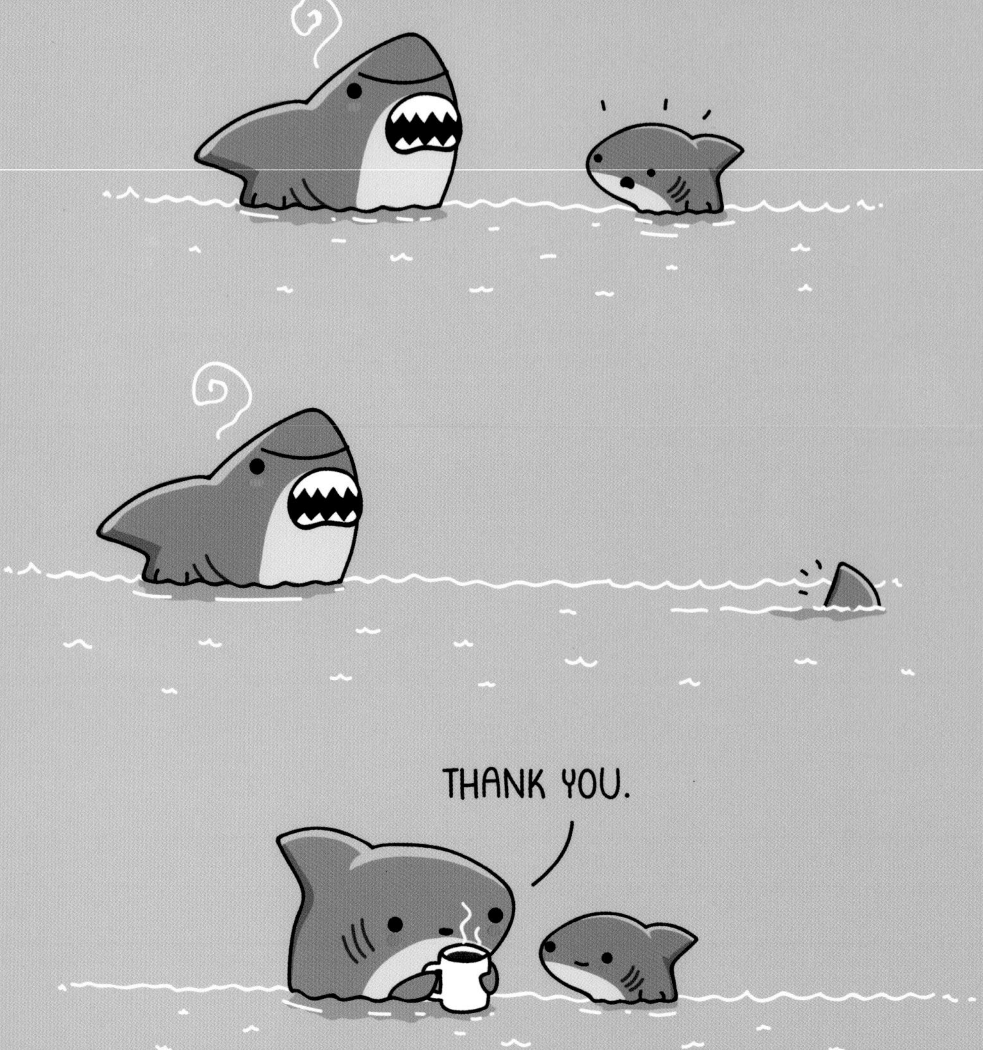
THANK YOU.

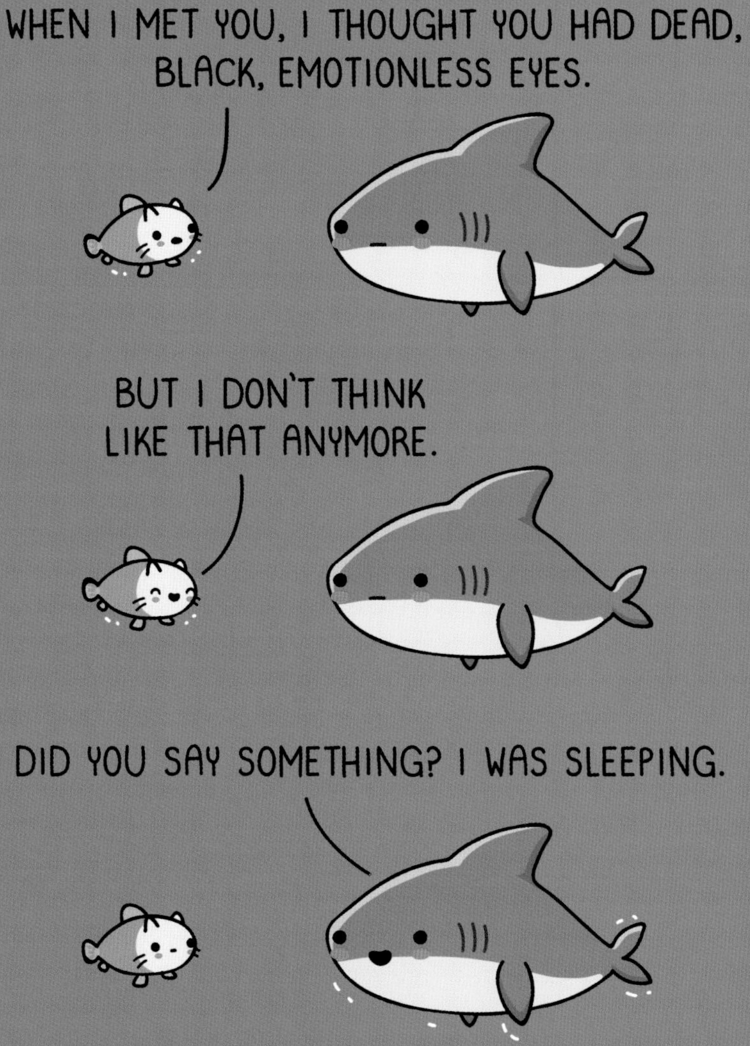
WHEN I MET YOU, I THOUGHT YOU HAD DEAD, BLACK, EMOTIONLESS EYES.
BUT I DON'T THINK LIKE THAT ANYMORE.
DID YOU SAY SOMETHING? I WAS SLEEPING.

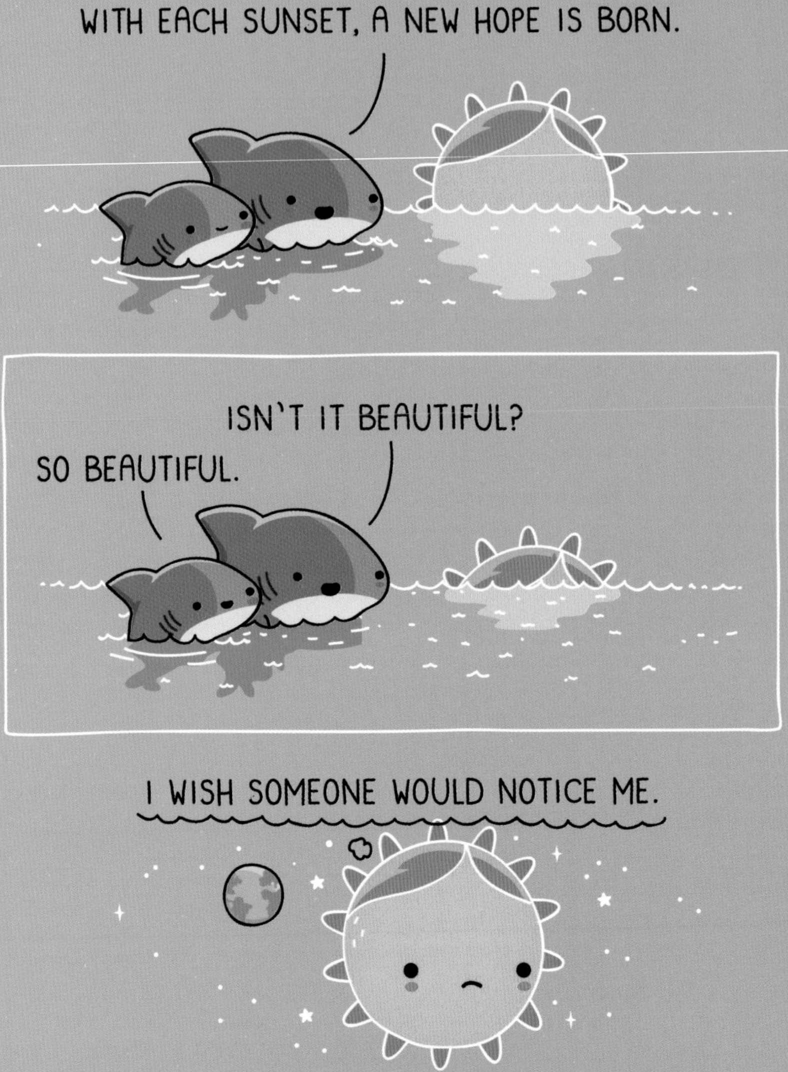

WITH EACH SUNSET, A NEW HOPE IS BORN.
ISN'T IT BEAUTIFUL?
SO BEAUTIFUL.
I WISH SOMEONE WOULD NOTICE ME.

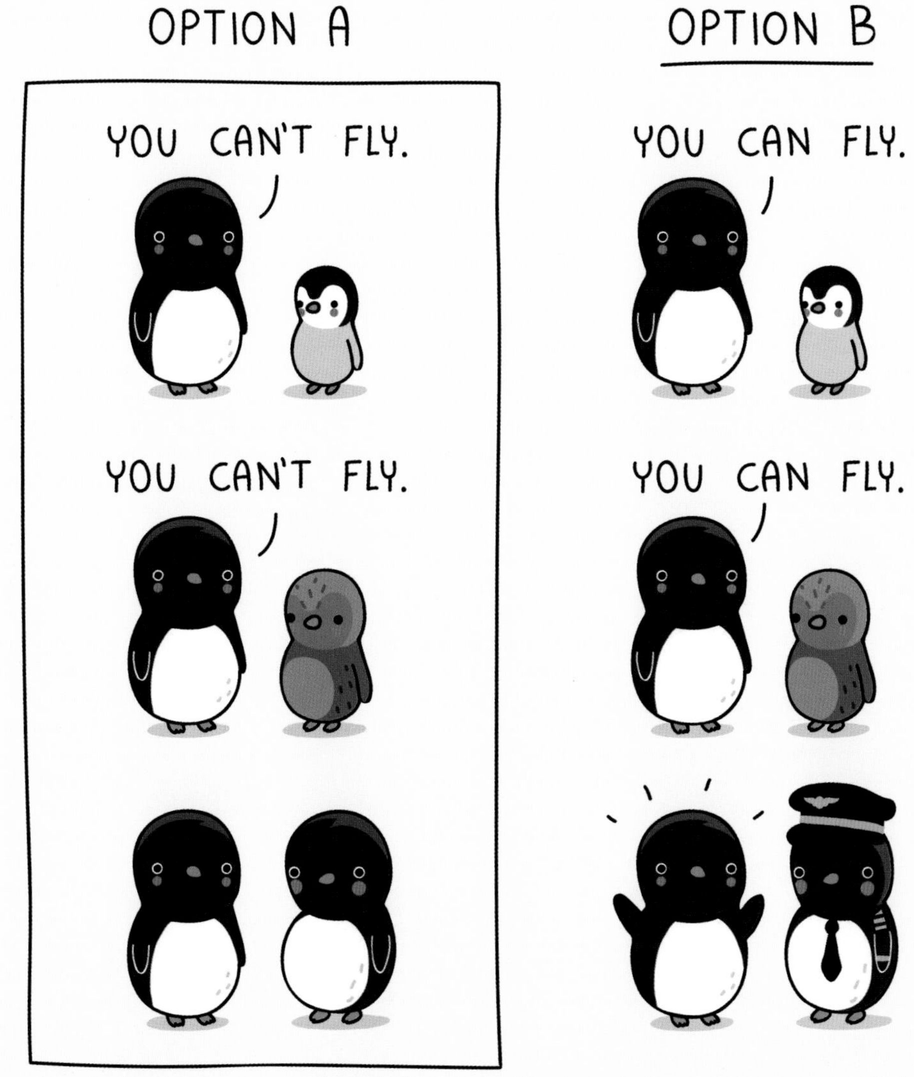
OPTION A
YOU CAN'T FLY.
YOU CAN'T FLY.
OPTION B
YOU CAN FLY.
YOU CAN FLY.

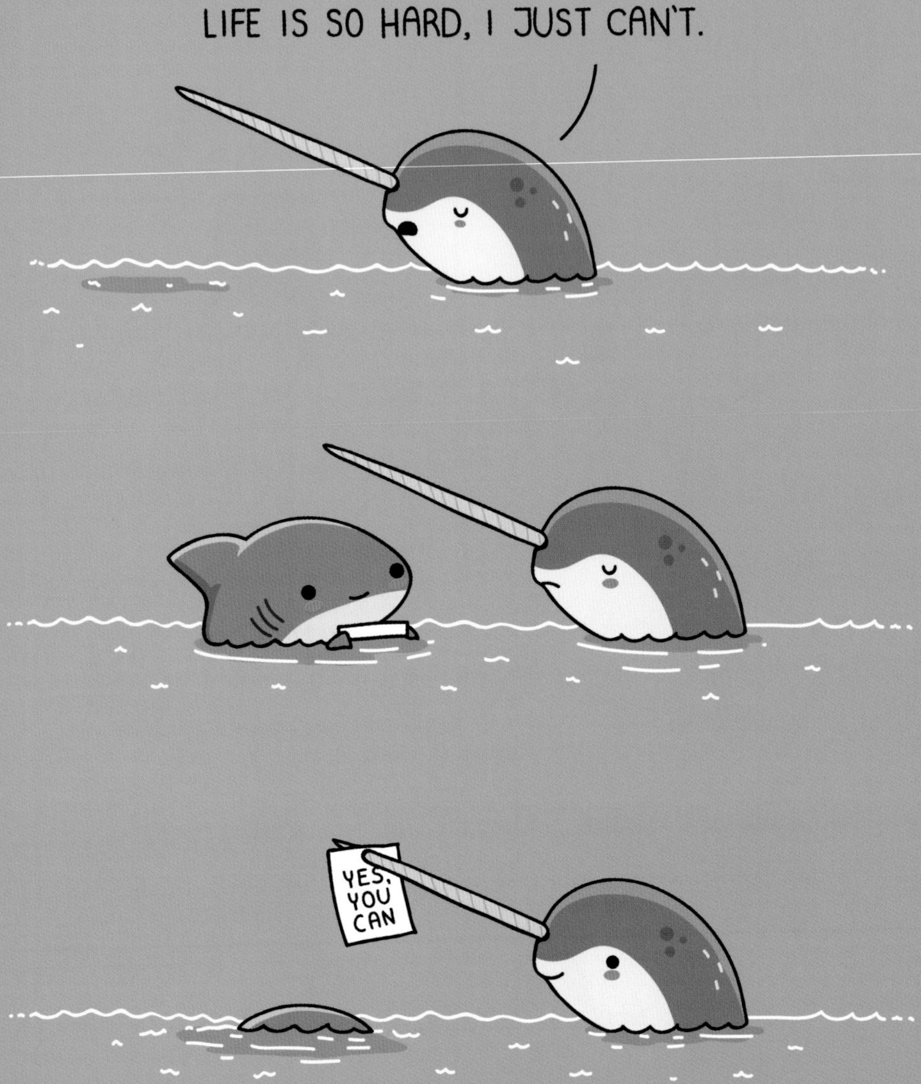
LIFE IS SO HARD, I JUST CAN'T.
YES, YOU CAN

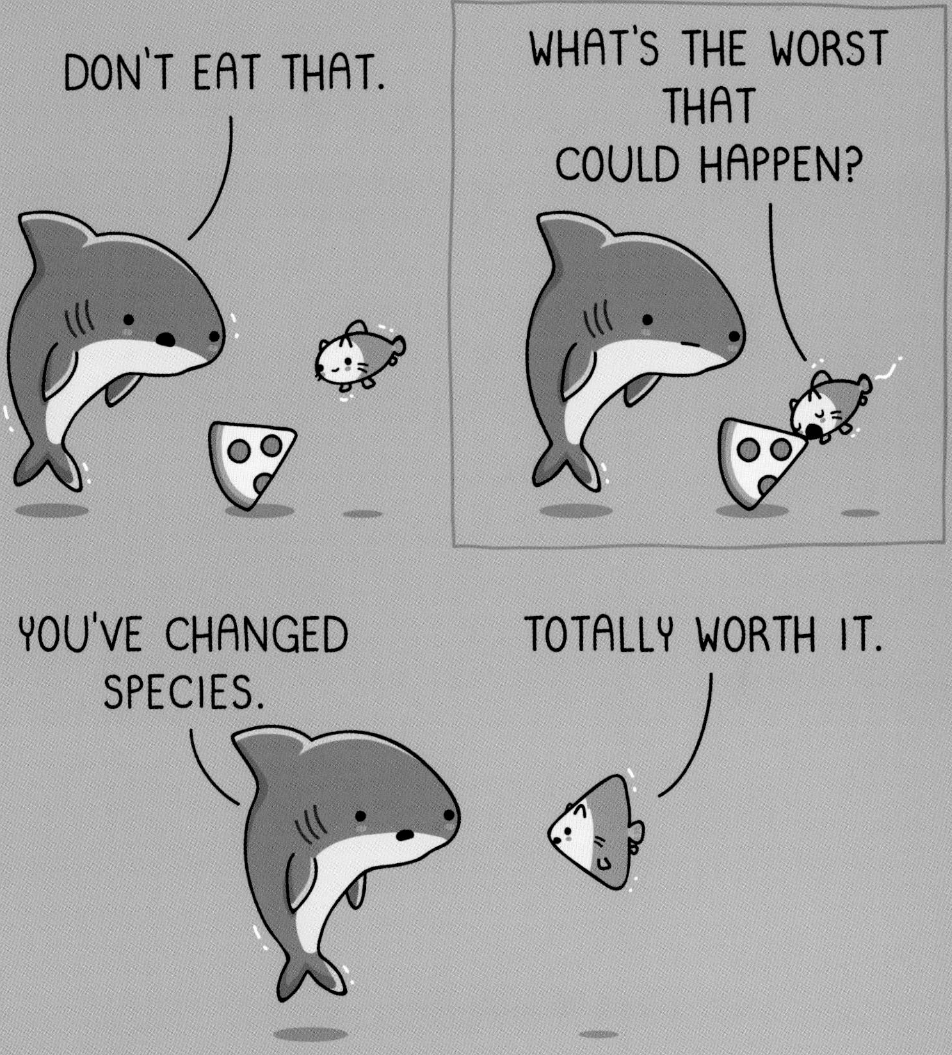
DON'T EAT THAT.
WHAT'S THE WORST THAT COULD HAPPEN?
YOU'VE CHANGED SPECIES.
TOTALLY WORTH IT.

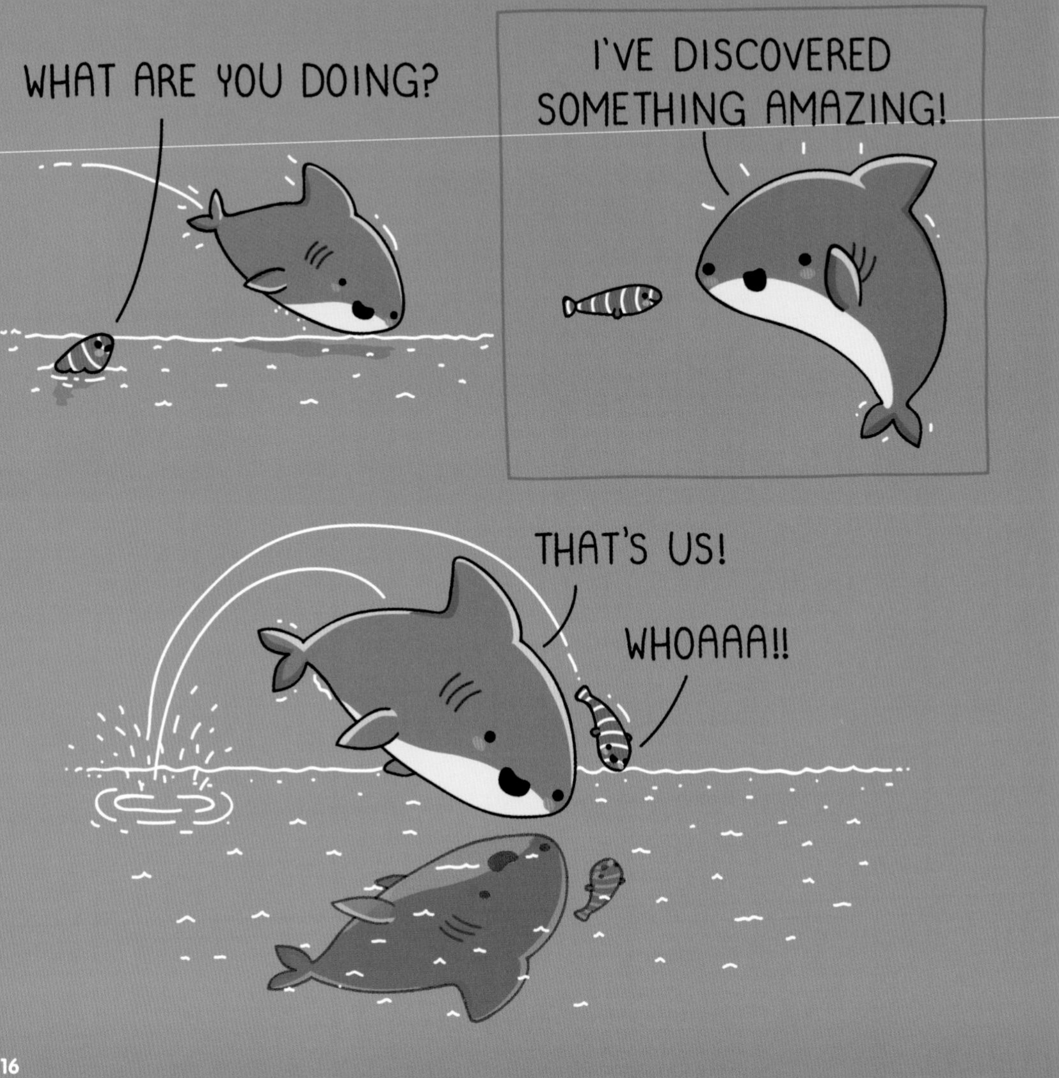
WHAT ARE YOU DOING?
I'VE DISCOVERED SOMETHING AMAZING!
THAT'S US!
WHOAAA!!

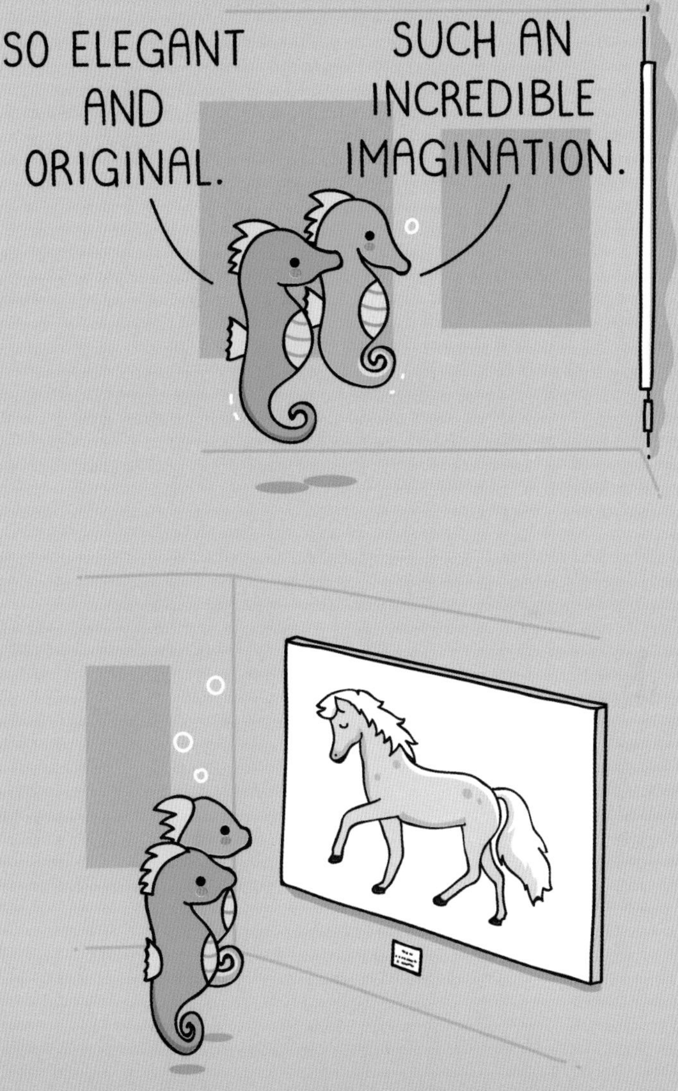
SO ELEGANT AND ORIGINAL.
SUCH AN INCREDIBLE IMAGINATION.

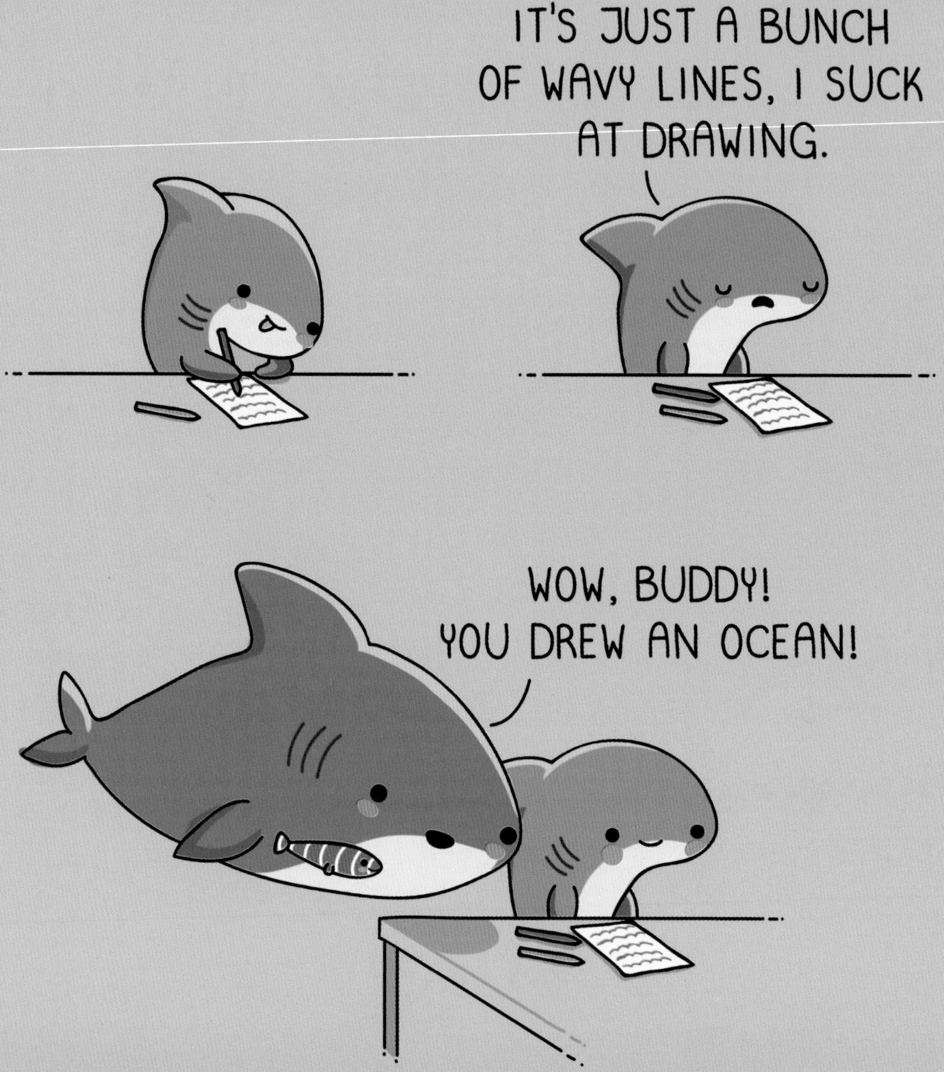
IT'S JUST A BUNCH OF WAVY LINES, I SUCK AT DRAWING.
WOW, BUDDY! YOU DREW AN OCEAN!

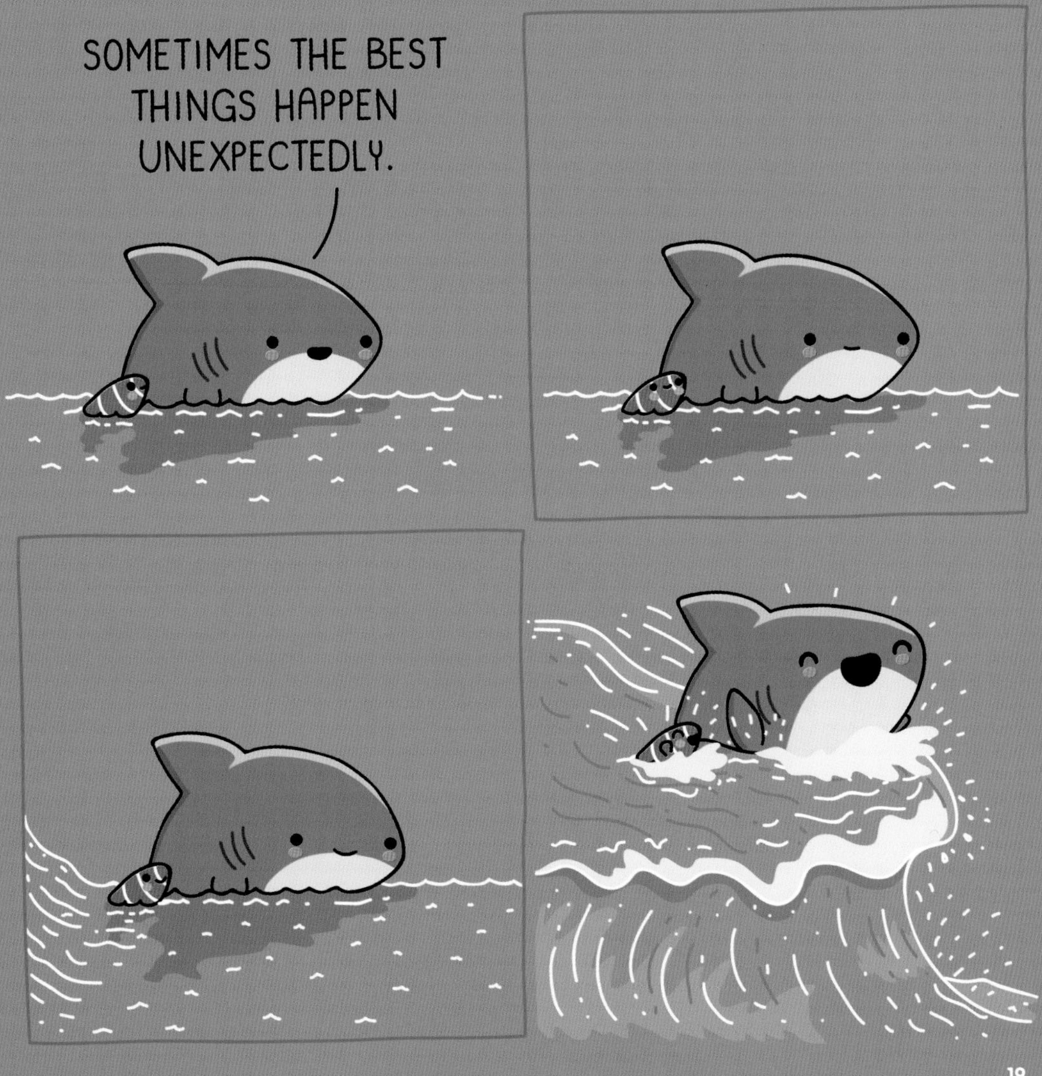
SOMETIMES THE BEST THINGS HAPPEN UNEXPECTEDLY.

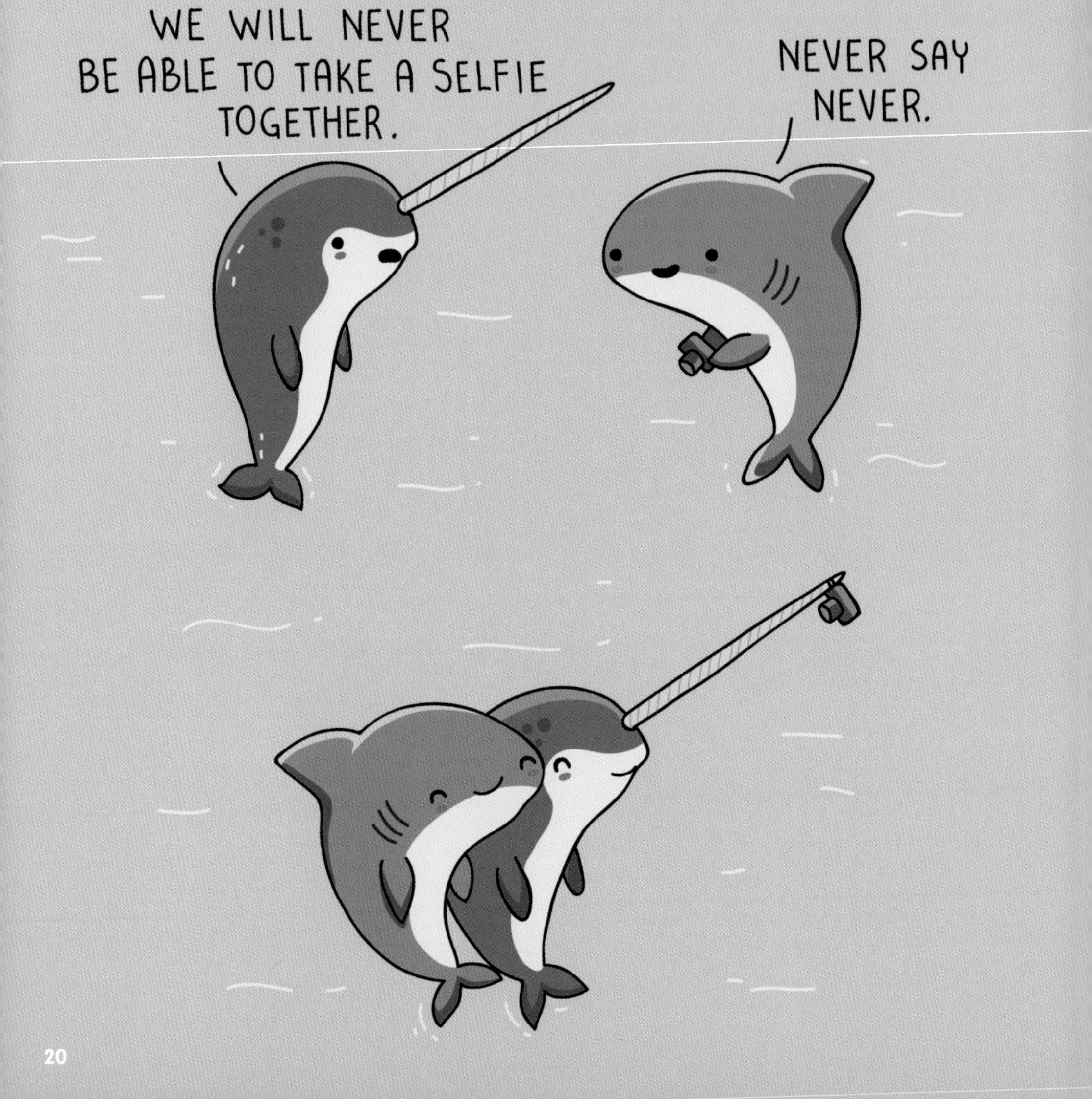
WE WILL NEVER BE ABLE TO TAKE A SELFIE TOGETHER.
NEVER SAY NEVER.

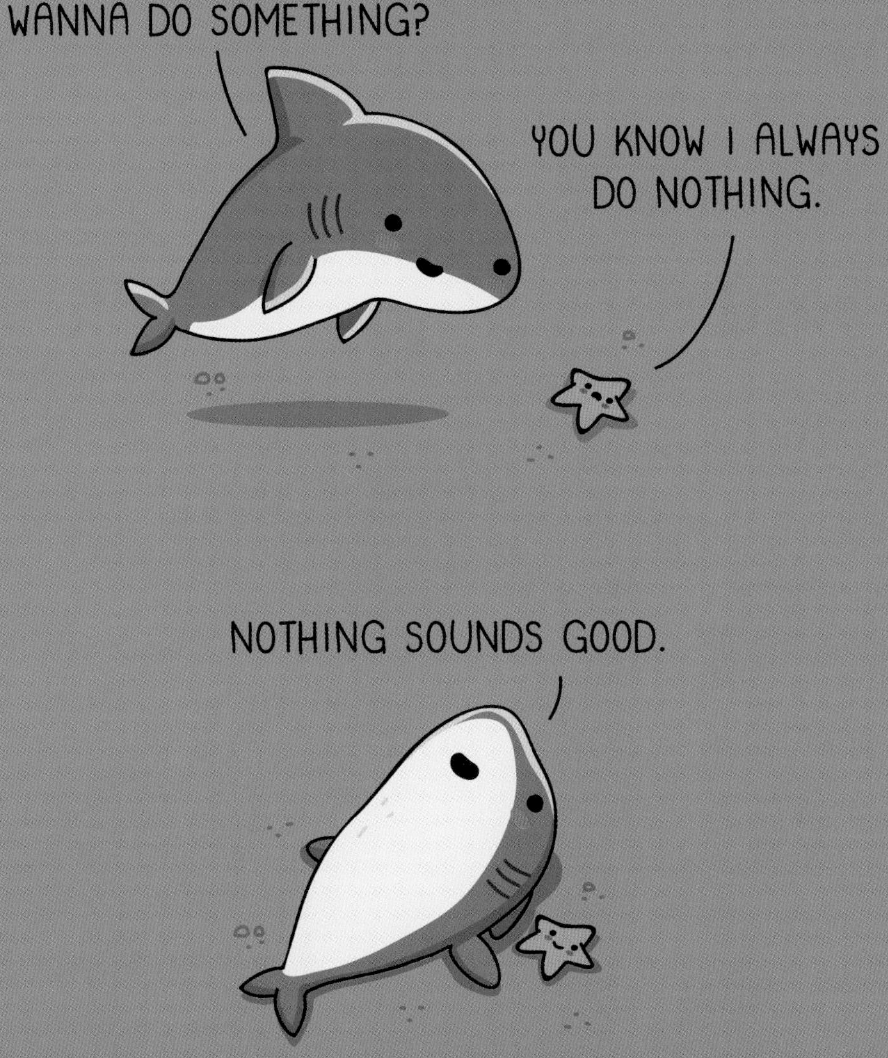
WANNA DO SOMETHING?
YOU KNOW I ALWAYS DO NOTHING.
NOTHING SOUNDS GOOD.

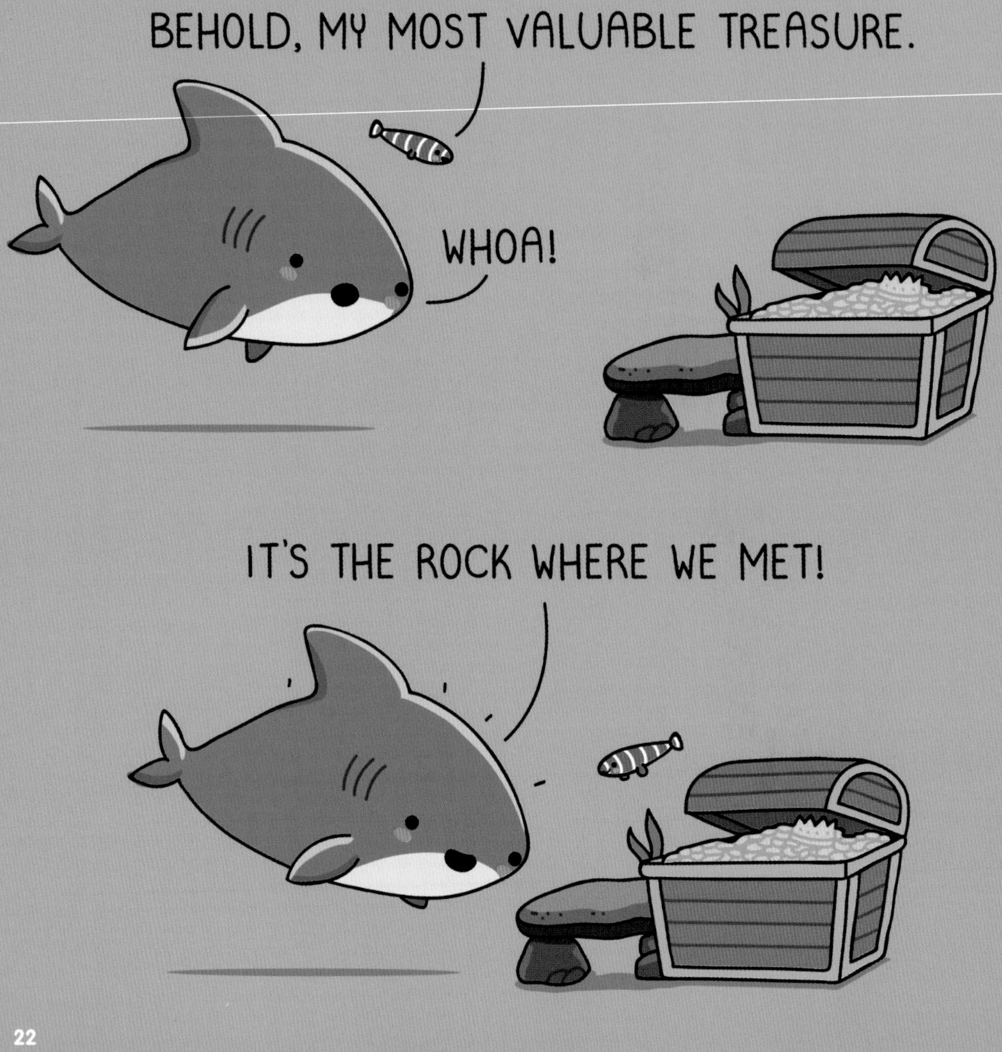
BEHOLD, MY MOST VALUABLE TREASURE.
WHOA!
IT'S THE ROCK WHERE WE MET!

WHAT ARE YOU DOING?

I TOTALLY MISREAD THE SITUATION.

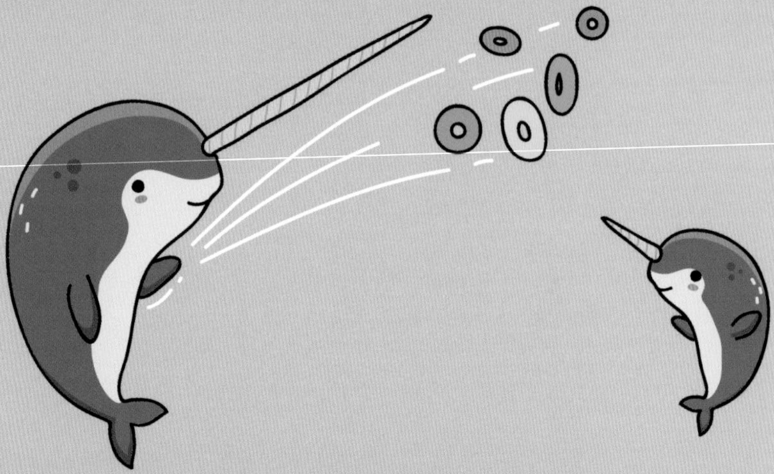

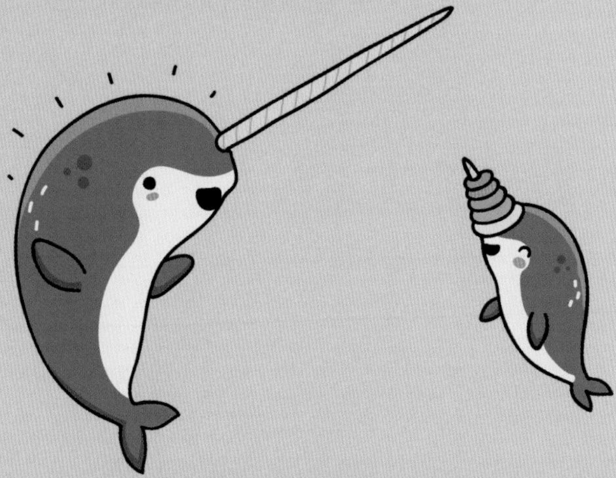

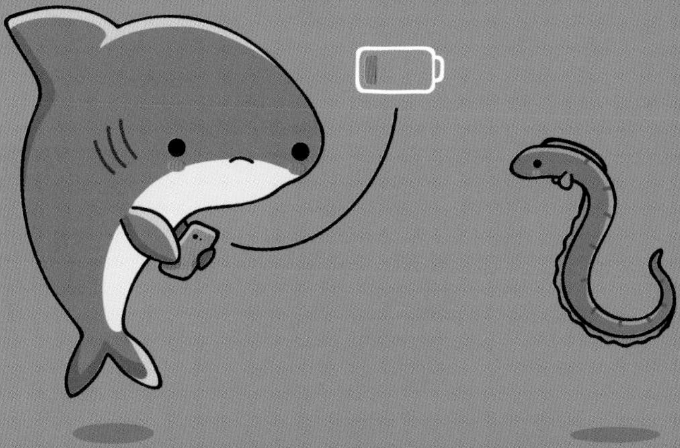

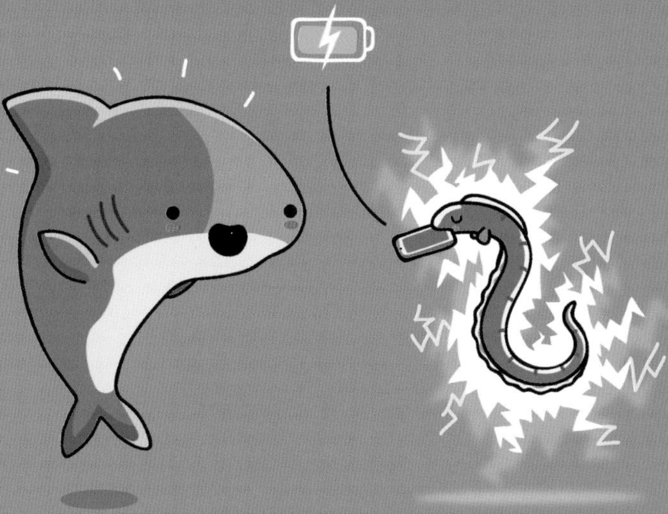

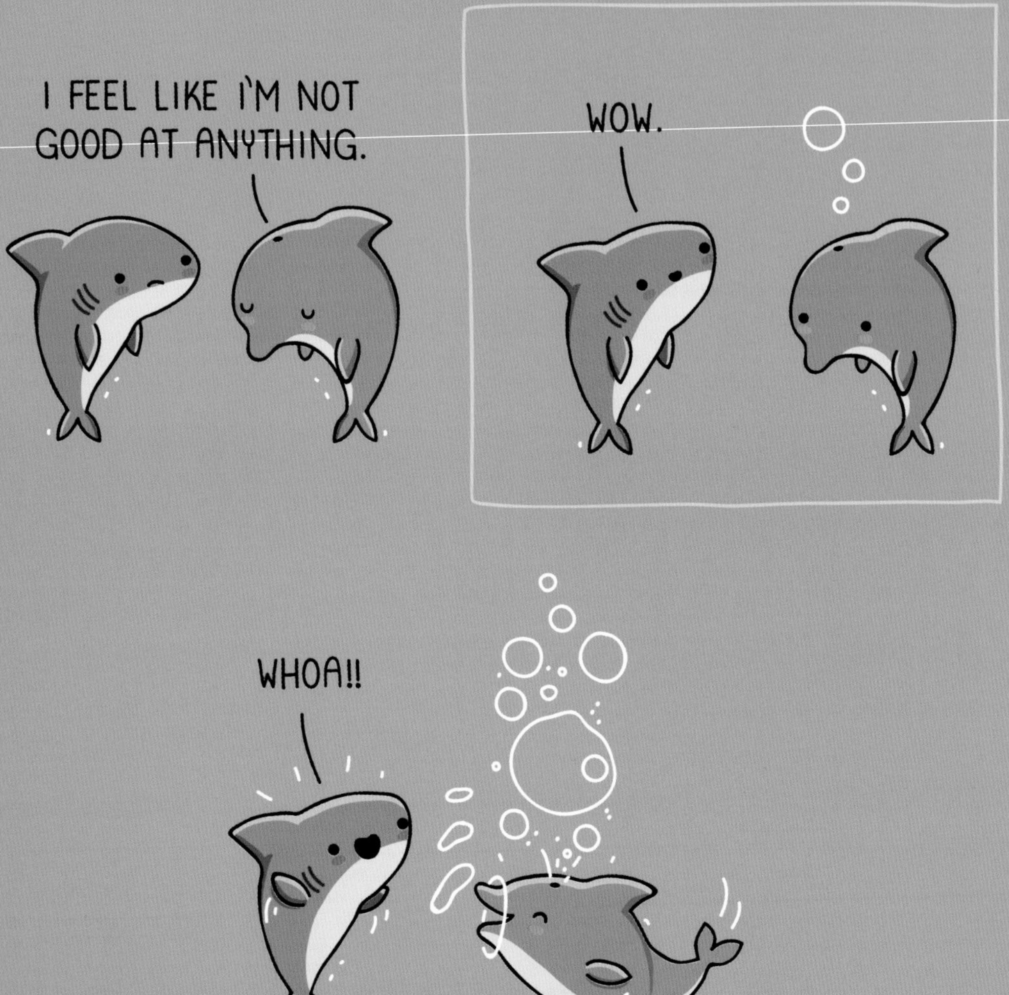

I FEEL LIKE I'M NOT GOOD AT ANYTHING.
WOW.
WHOA!!

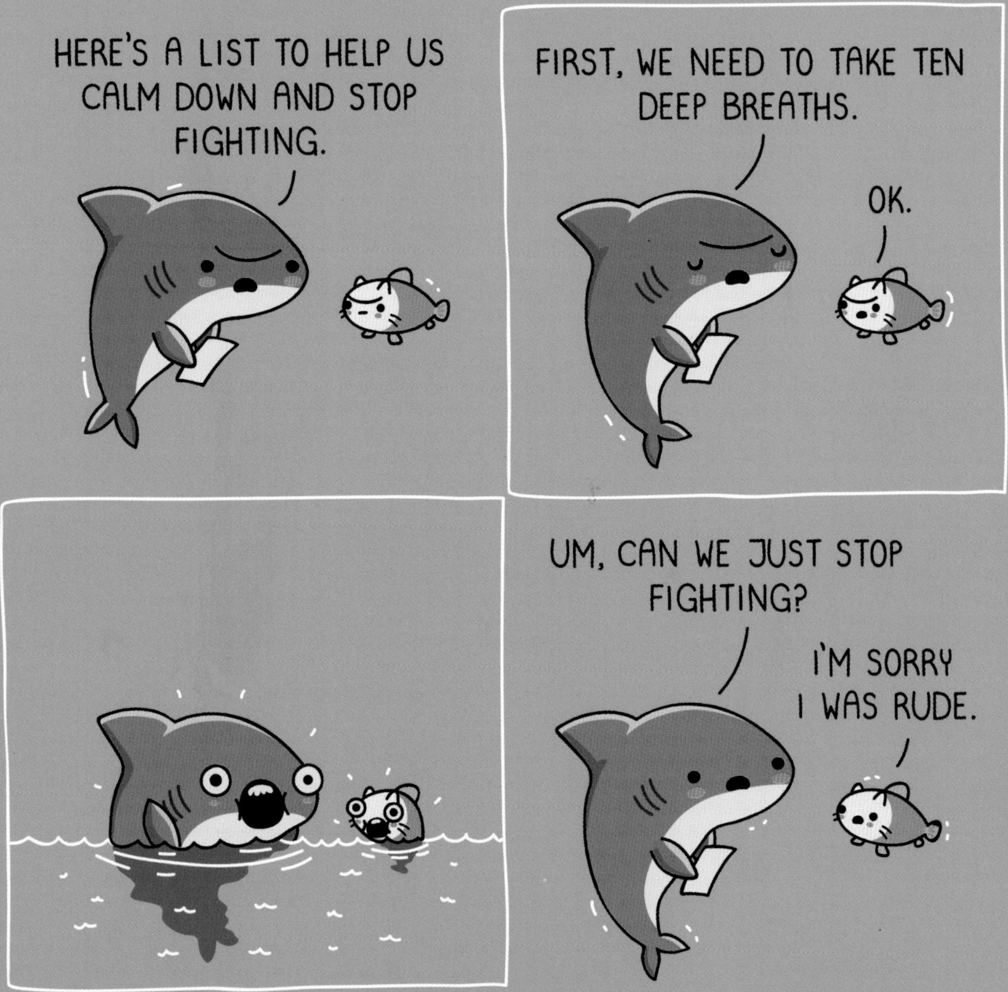
HERE'S A LIST TO HELP US CALM DOWN AND STOP FIGHTING.
FIRST, WE NEED TO TAKE TEN DEEP BREATHS.
OK.
UM, CAN WE JUST STOP FIGHTING?
I'M SORRY I WAS RUDE.

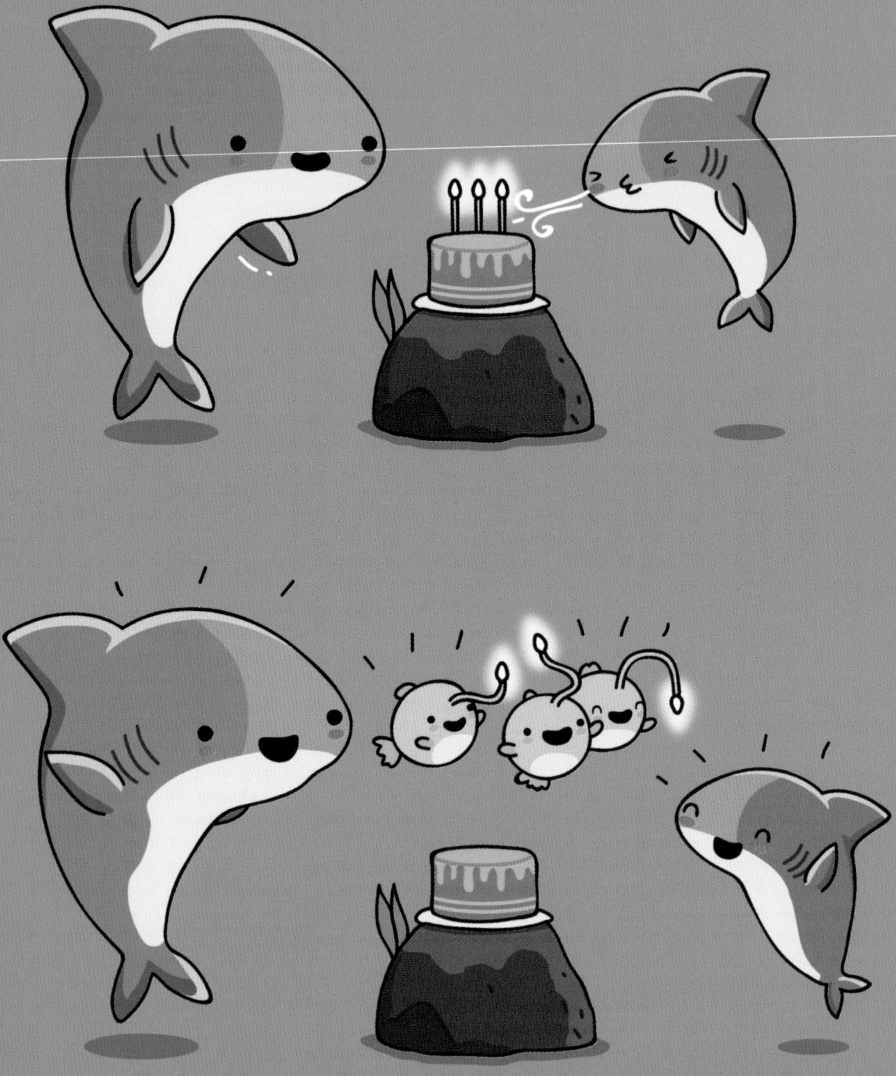

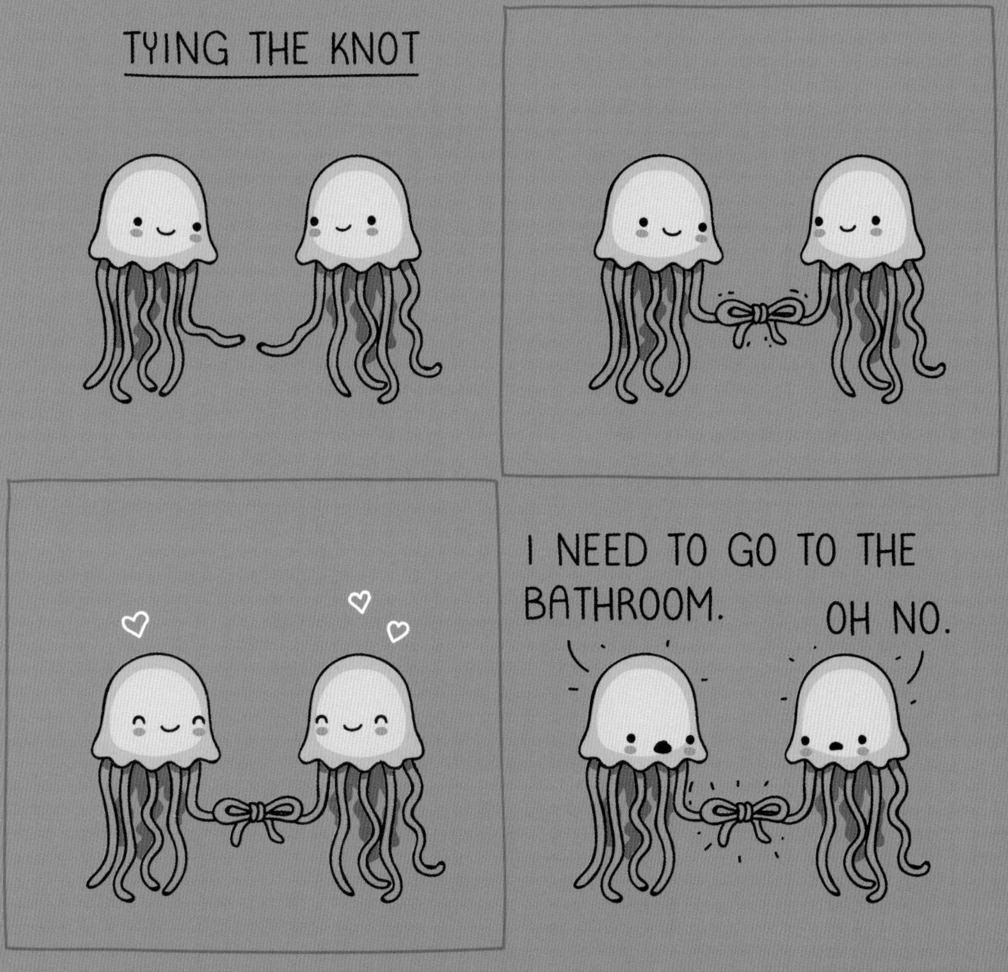
TYING THE KNOT
I NEED TO GO TO THE BATHROOM.
OH NO.

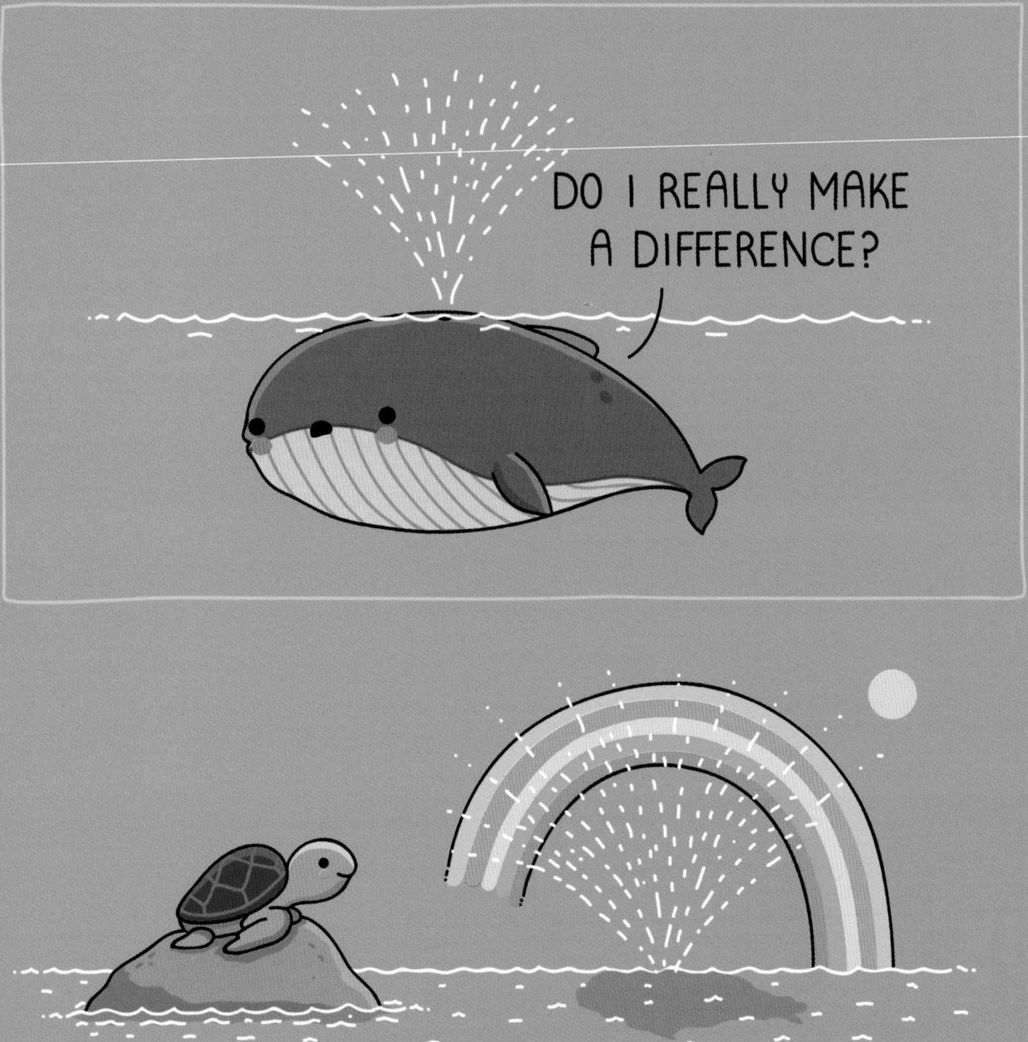
DO I REALLY MAKE A DIFFERENCE?

CAN WE SWITCH?
THIS IS NOT MY ANGLE.

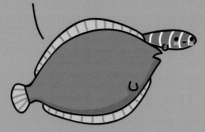

YOU CAN TAKE THE
PHOTO NOW.

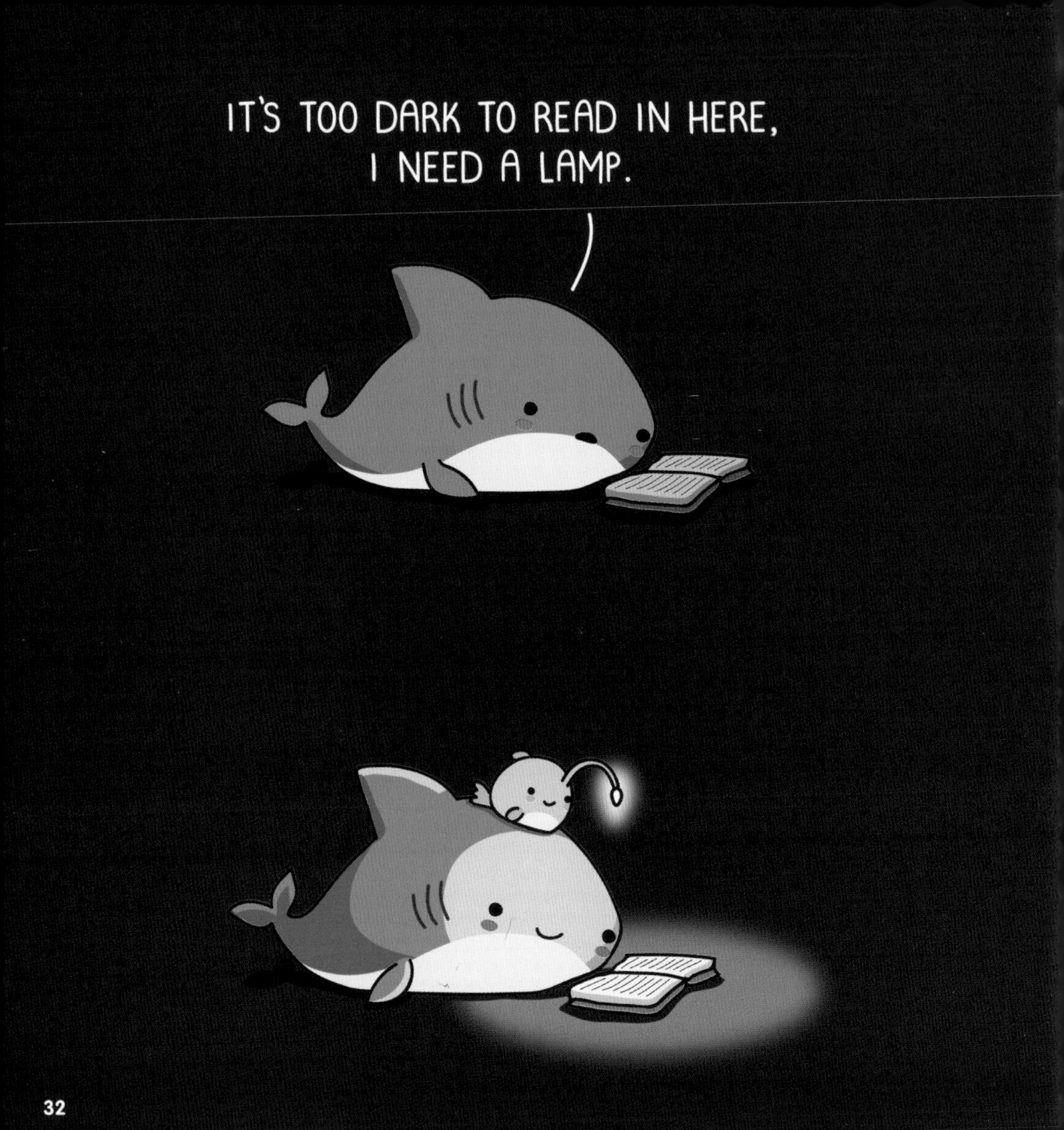
IT'S TOO DARK TO READ IN HERE,
I NEED A LAMP.

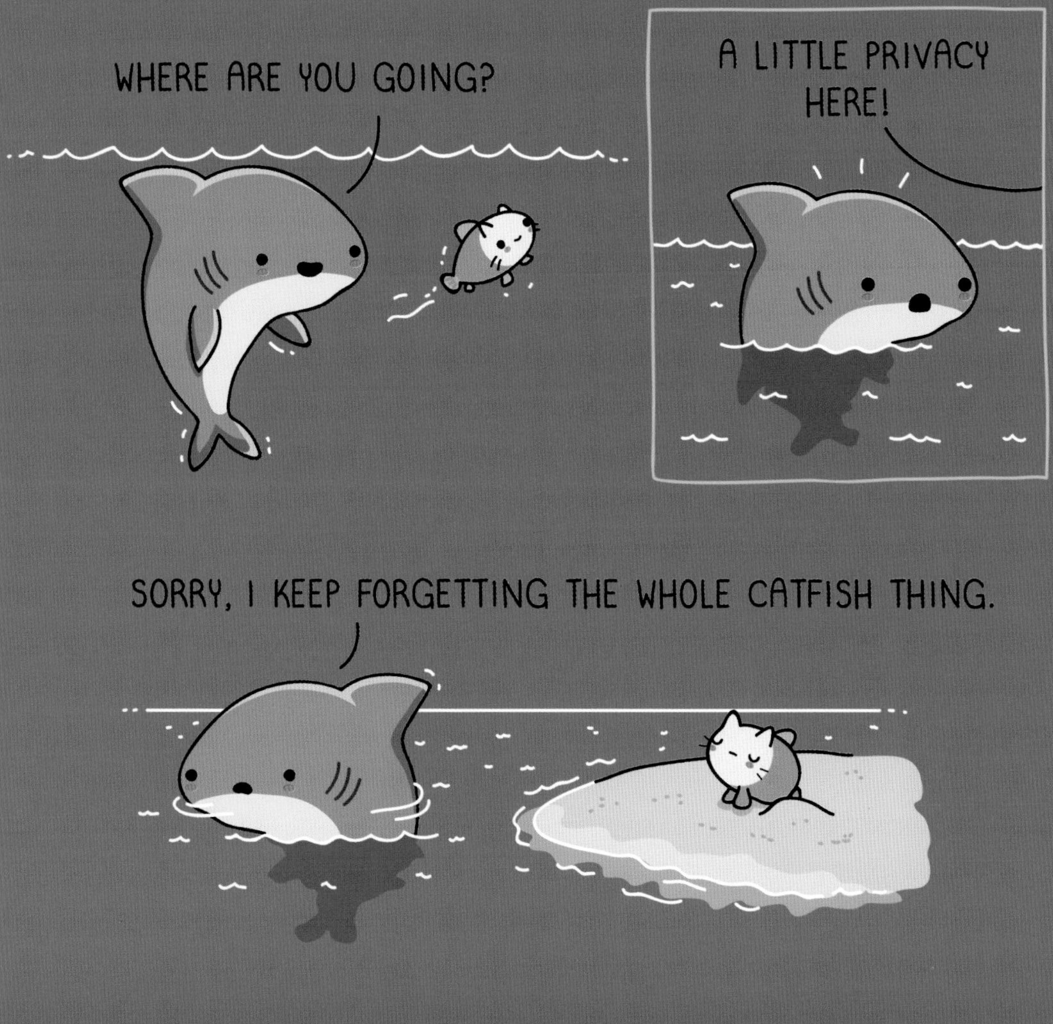

WHERE ARE YOU GOING?
A LITTLE PRIVACY HERE!
SORRY, I KEEP FORGETTING THE WHOLE CATFISH THING.

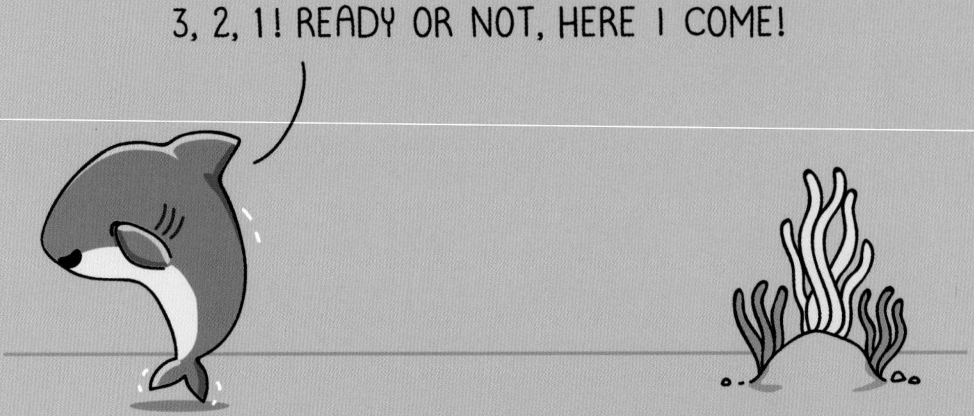
3, 2, 1! READY OR NOT, HERE I COME!

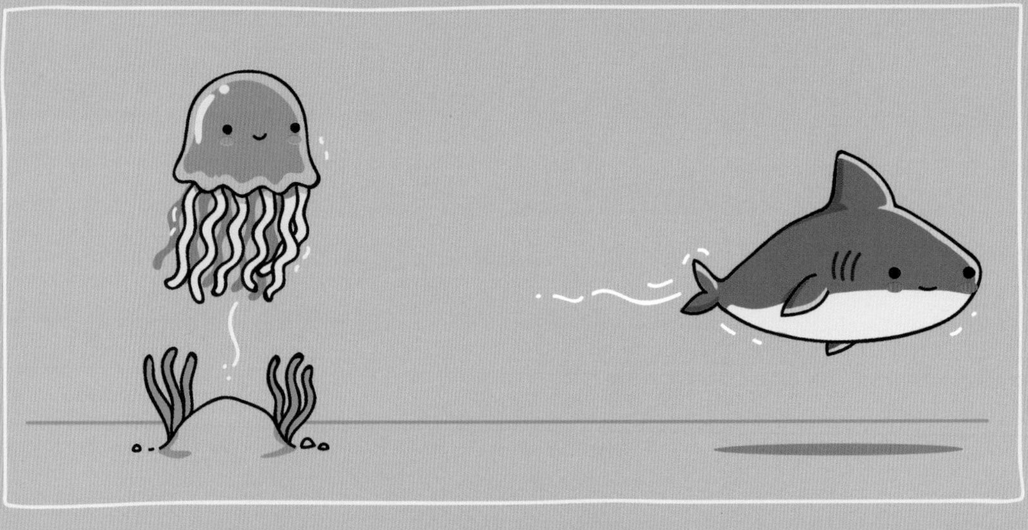

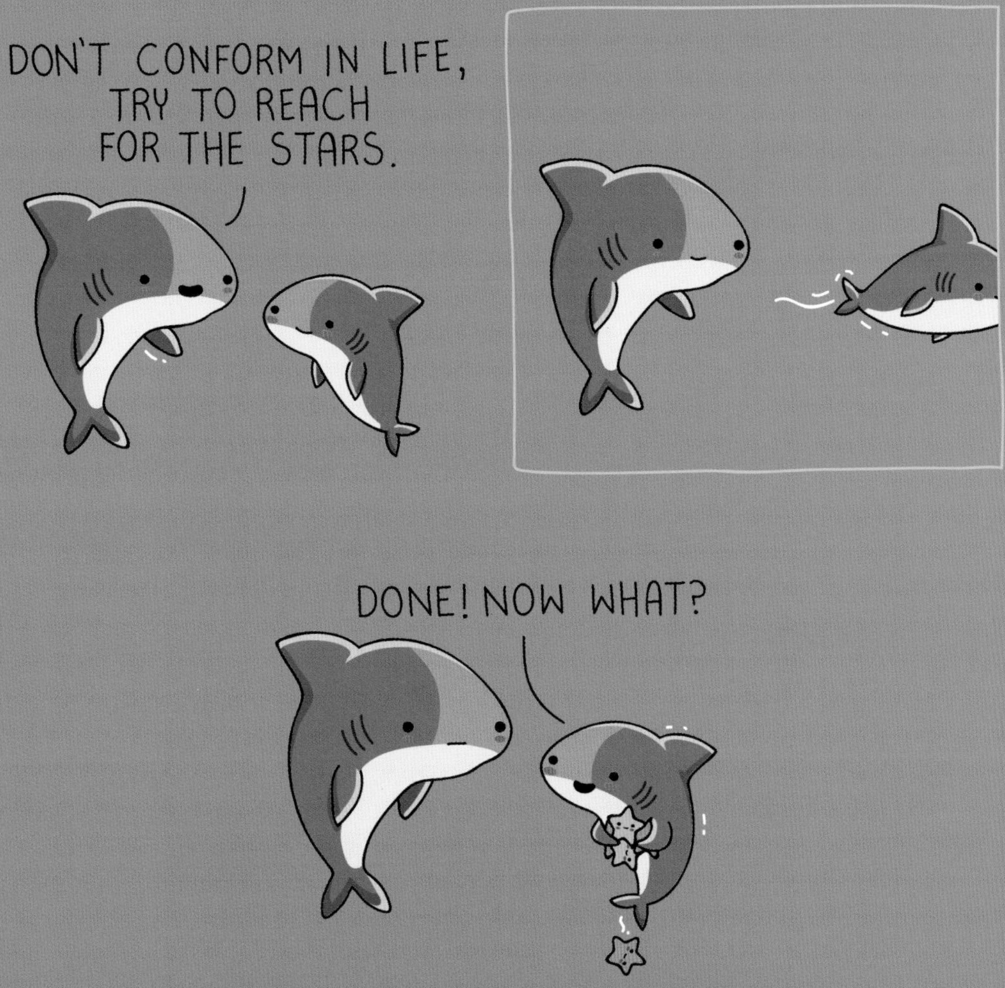
DON'T CONFORM IN LIFE, TRY TO REACH FOR THE STARS.
DONE! NOW WHAT?

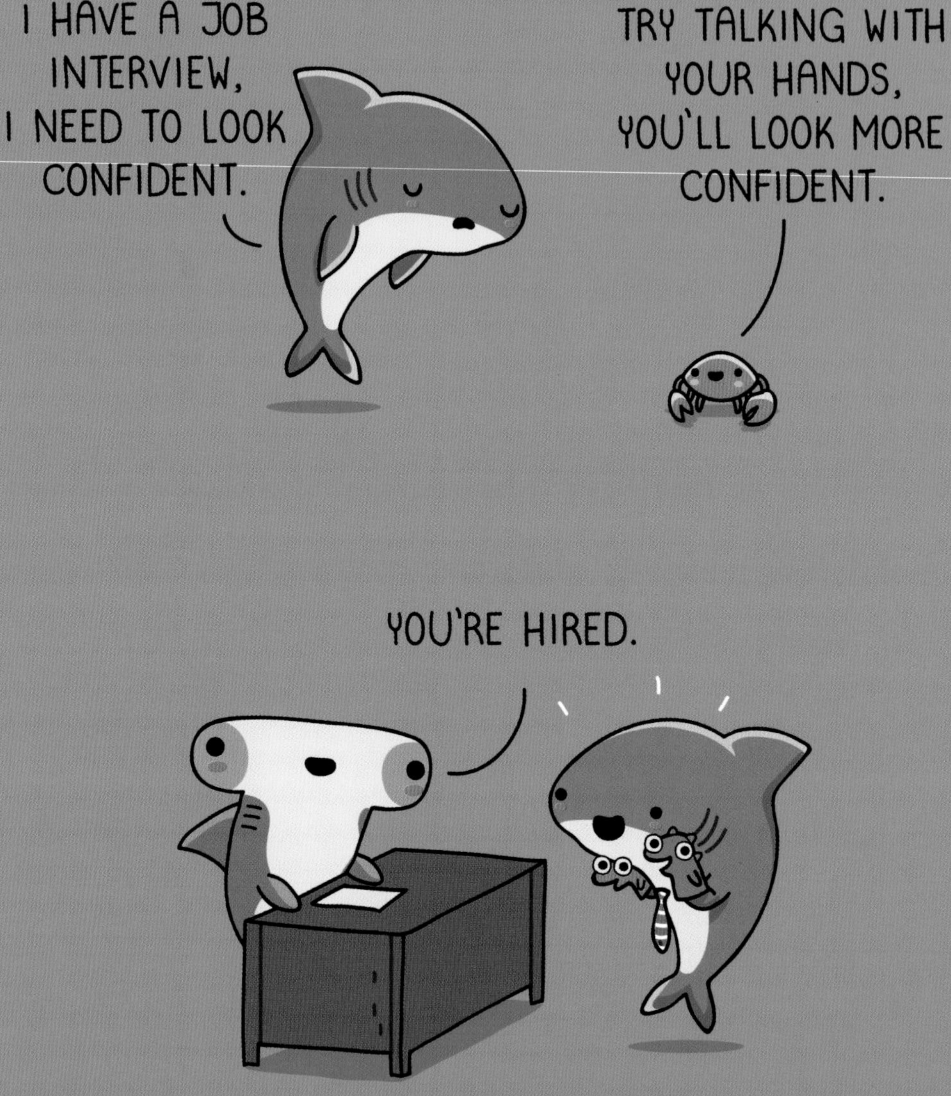
I HAVE A JOB INTERVIEW, I NEED TO LOOK CONFIDENT.
TRY TALKING WITH YOUR HANDS, YOU'LL LOOK MORE CONFIDENT.
YOU'RE HIRED.

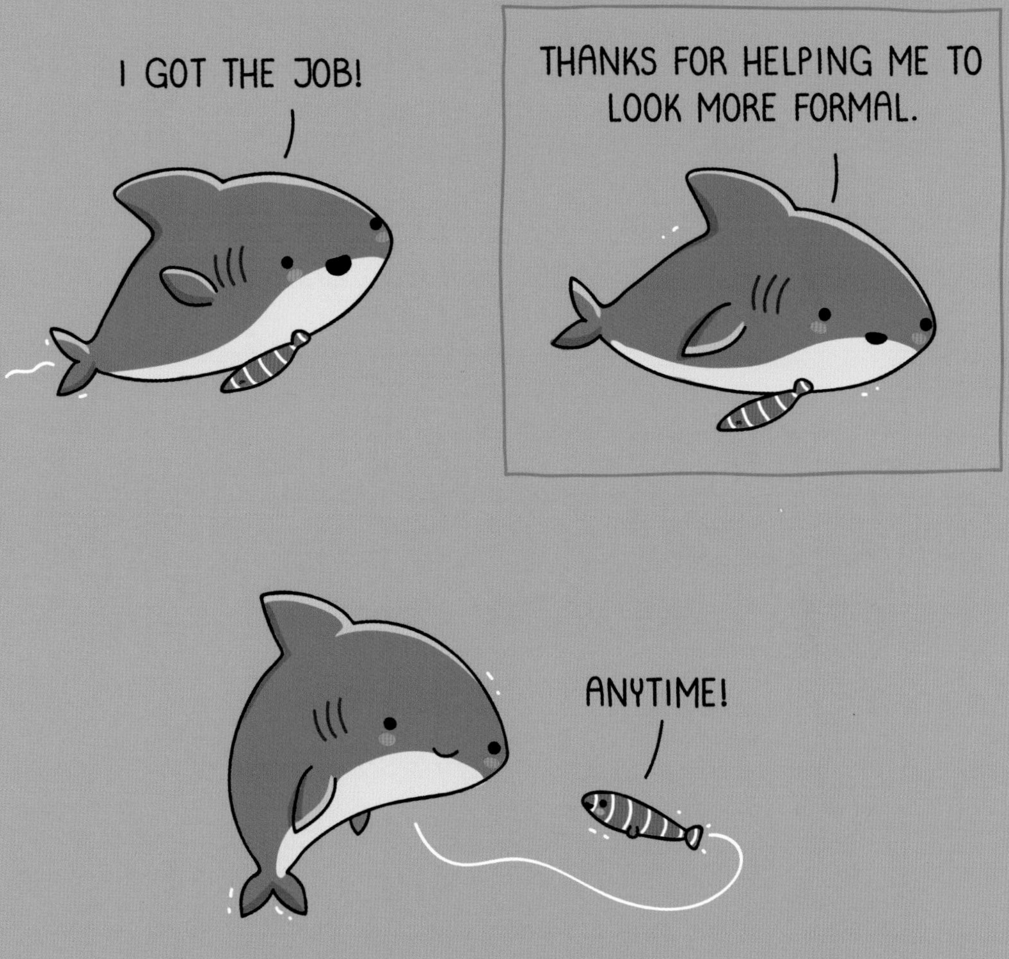
I GOT THE JOB!
THANKS FOR HELPING ME TO LOOK MORE FORMAL.
ANYTIME!

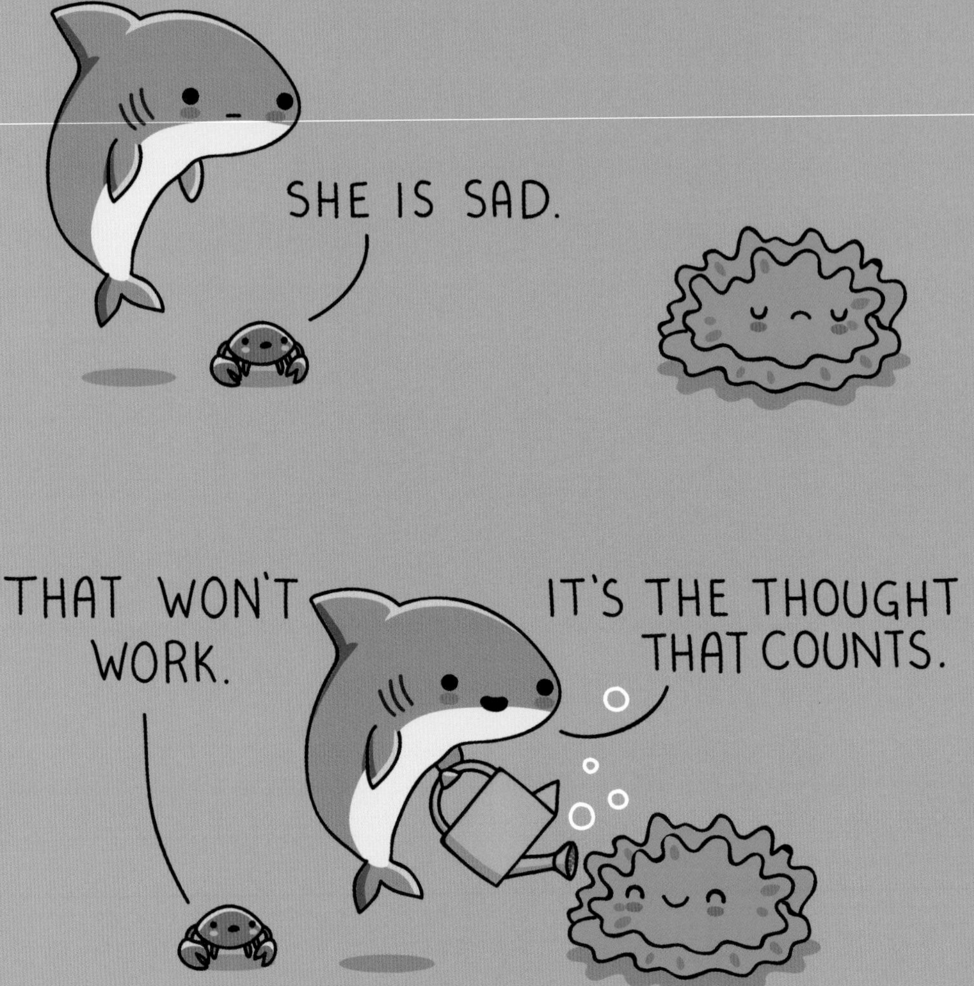
SHE IS SAD.
THAT WON'T WORK.
IT'S THE THOUGHT THAT COUNTS.

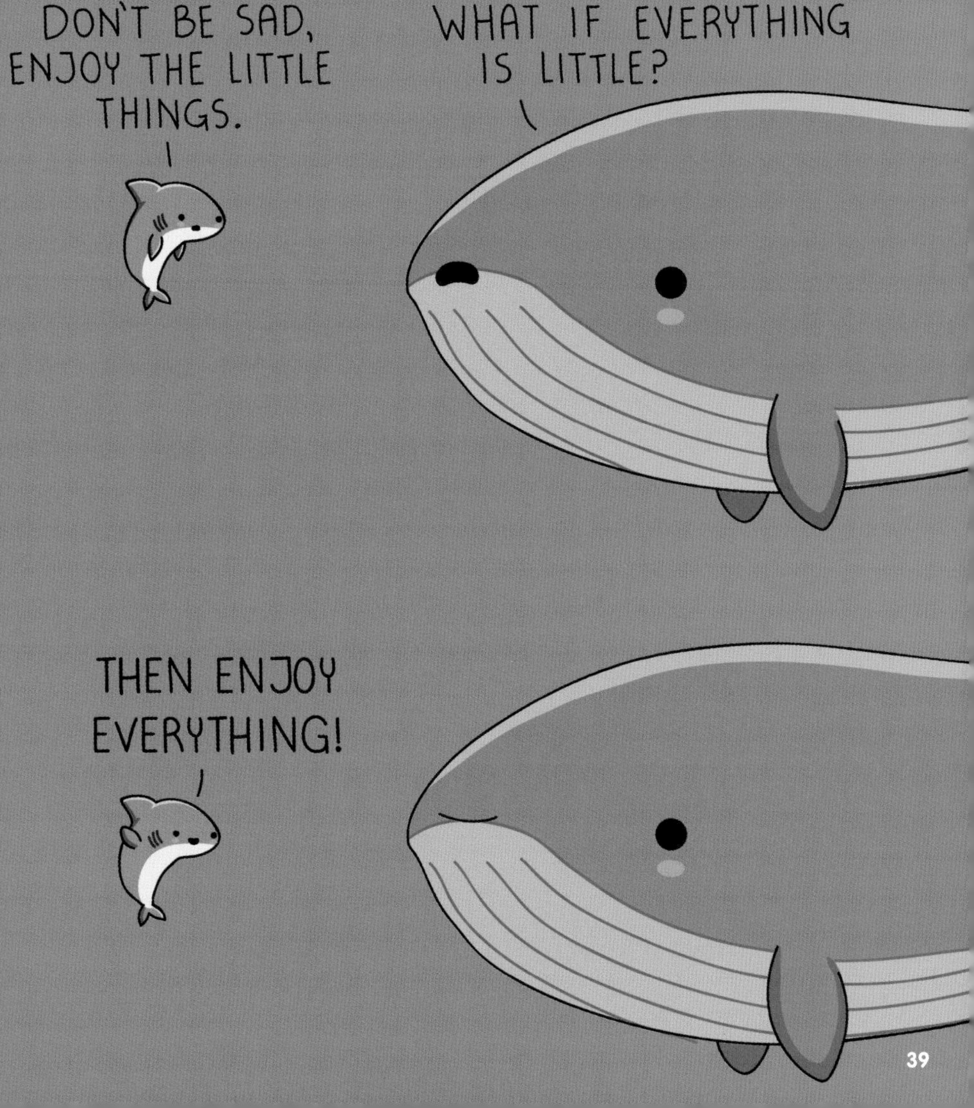
DON'T BE SAD, ENJOY THE LITTLE THINGS.
WHAT IF EVERYTHING IS LITTLE?
THEN ENJOY EVERYTHING!

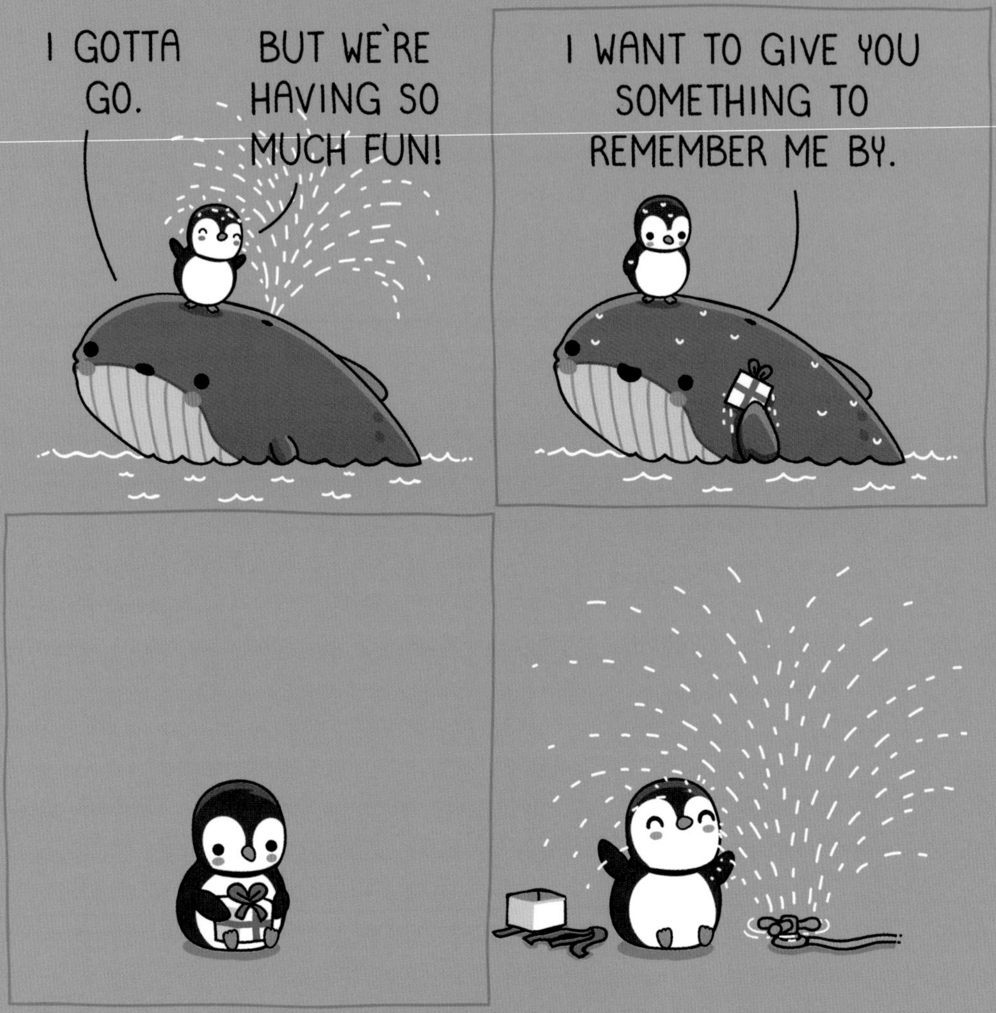
I GOTTA GO.
BUT WE'RE HAVING SO MUCH FUN!
I WANT TO GIVE YOU SOMETHING TO REMEMBER ME BY.

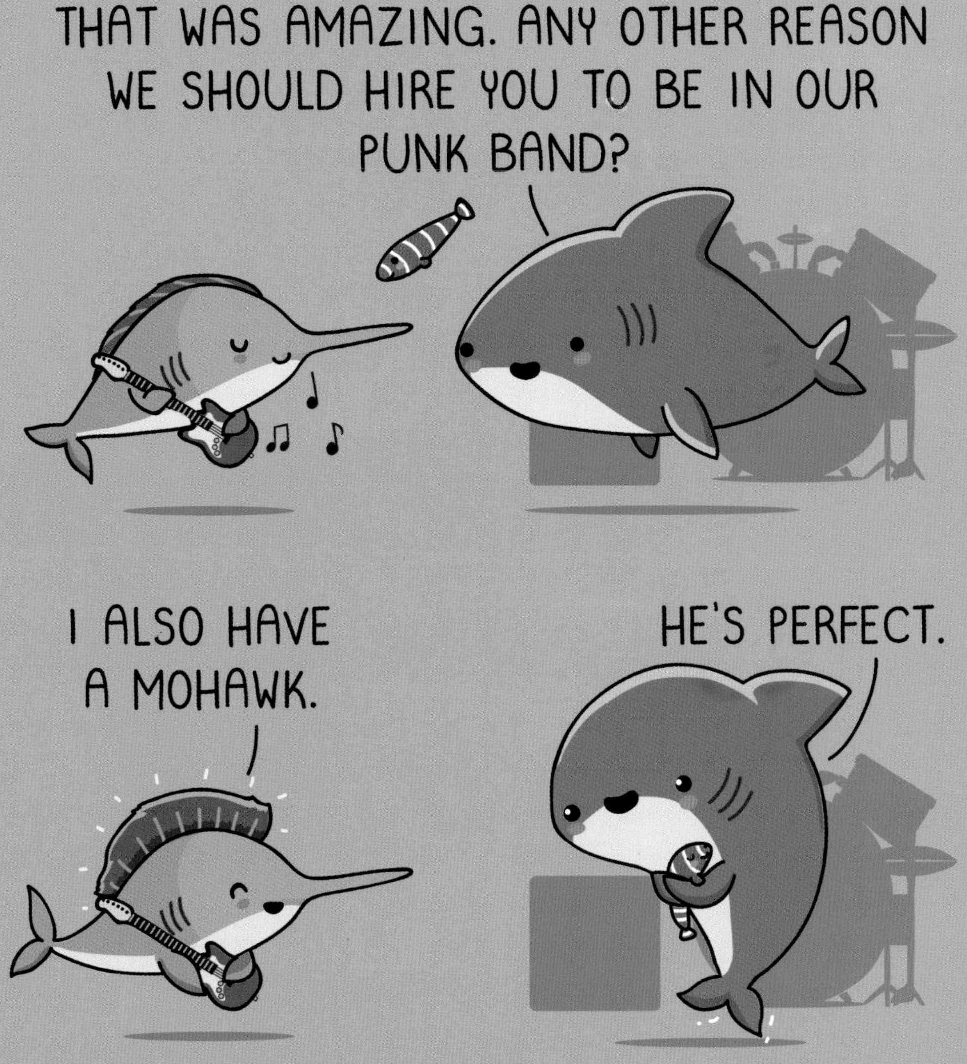
THAT WAS AMAZING. ANY OTHER REASON WE SHOULD HIRE YOU TO BE IN OUR PUNK BAND?
I ALSO HAVE A MOHAWK.
HE'S PERFECT.

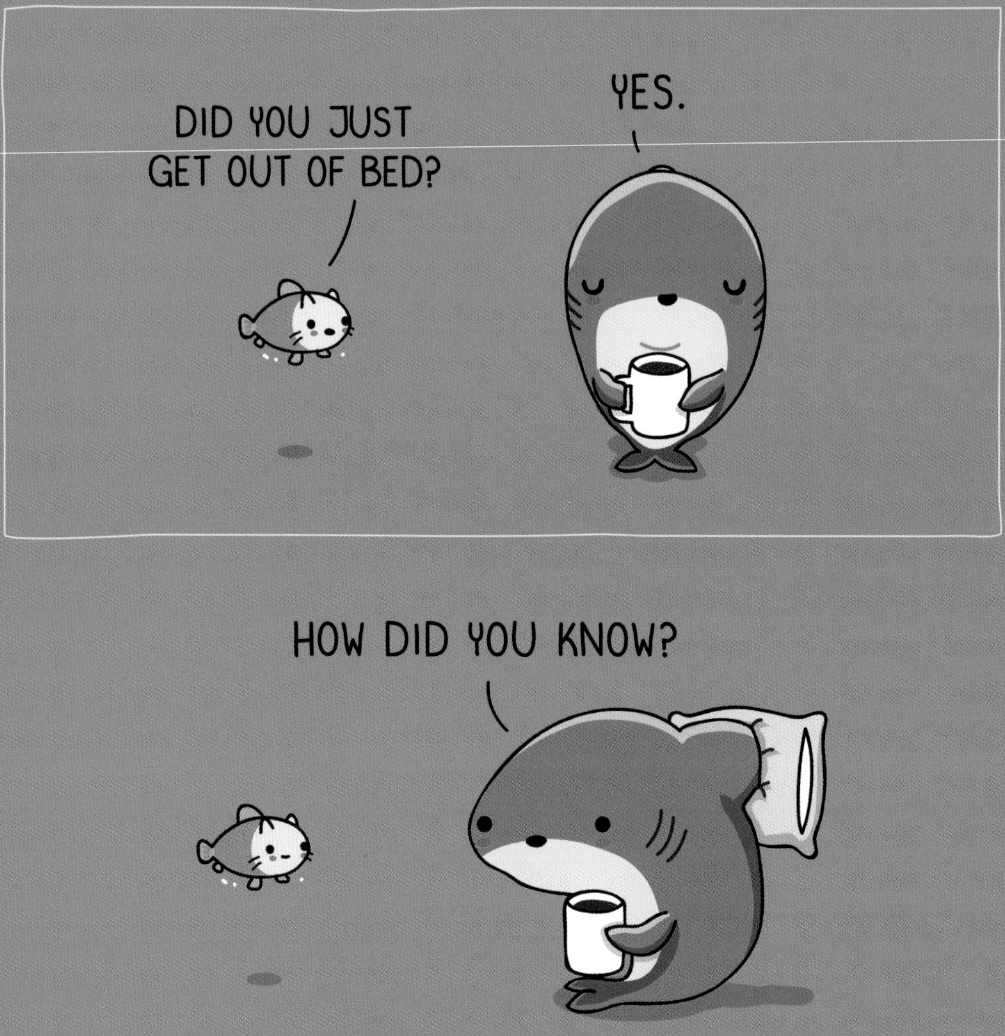
DID YOU JUST GET OUT OF BED?
YES.
HOW DID YOU KNOW?

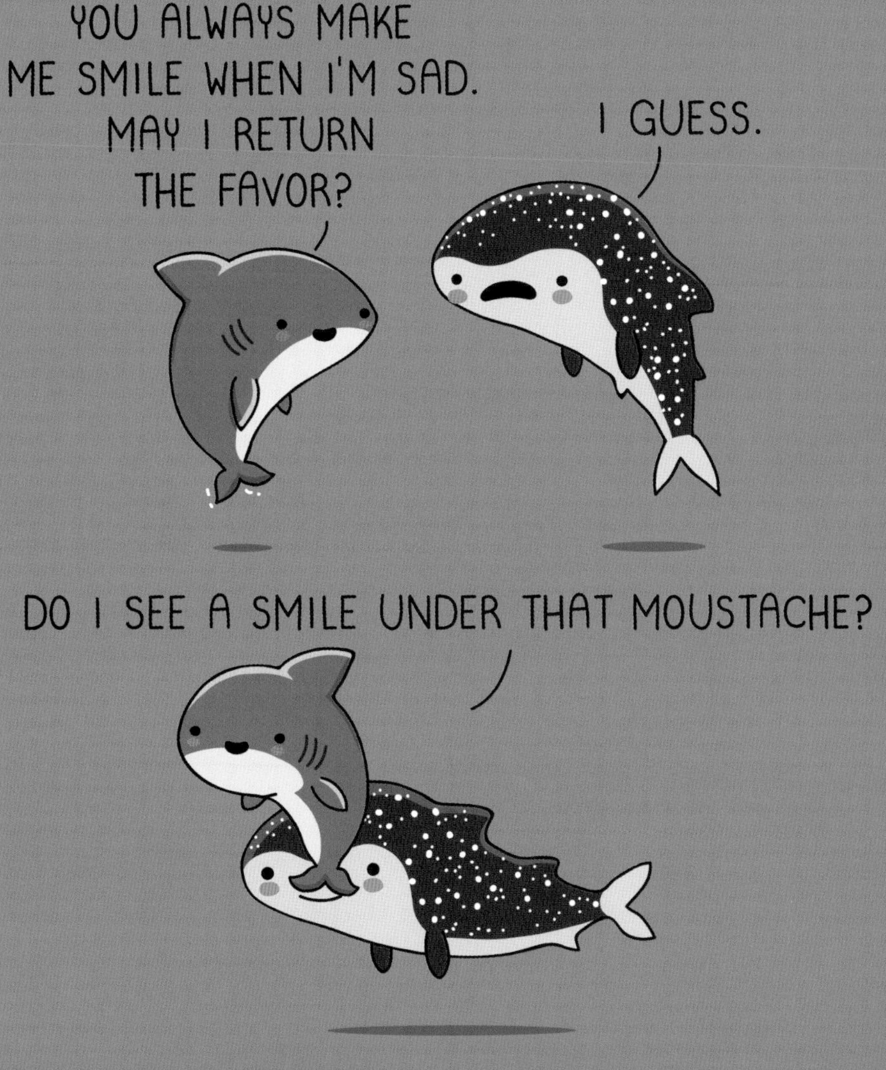
YOU ALWAYS MAKE ME SMILE WHEN I'M SAD. MAY I RETURN THE FAVOR?
I GUESS.
DO I SEE A SMILE UNDER THAT MOUSTACHE?

ONE DAY YOU'RE
ALONE.

THEN SOMEONE SPECIAL
GIFTS YOU A ROCK.

SO YOU CAN PLAY HOPSCOTCH.

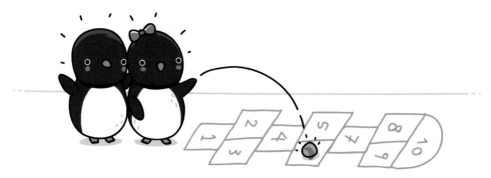

OK, THAT IS SCARY, I WON'T DO IT AGAIN!

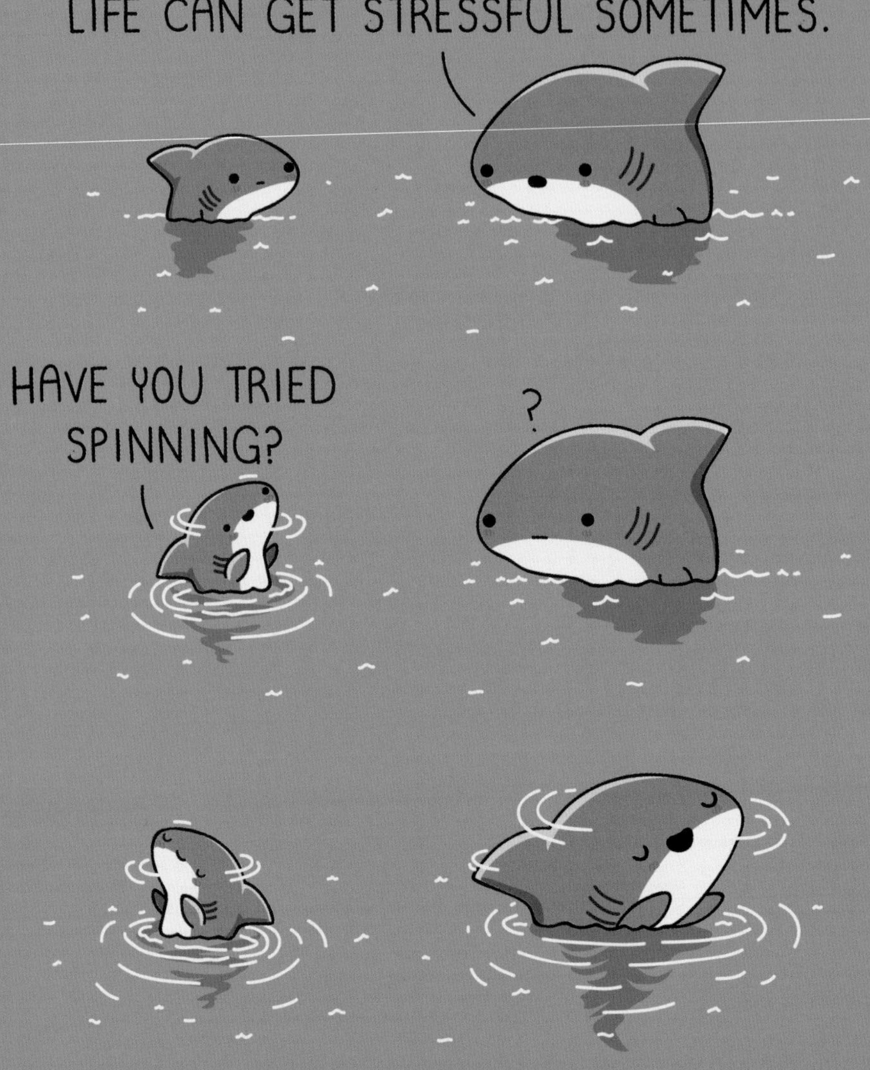
LIFE CAN GET STRESSFUL SOMETIMES.
HAVE YOU TRIED SPINNING?
?

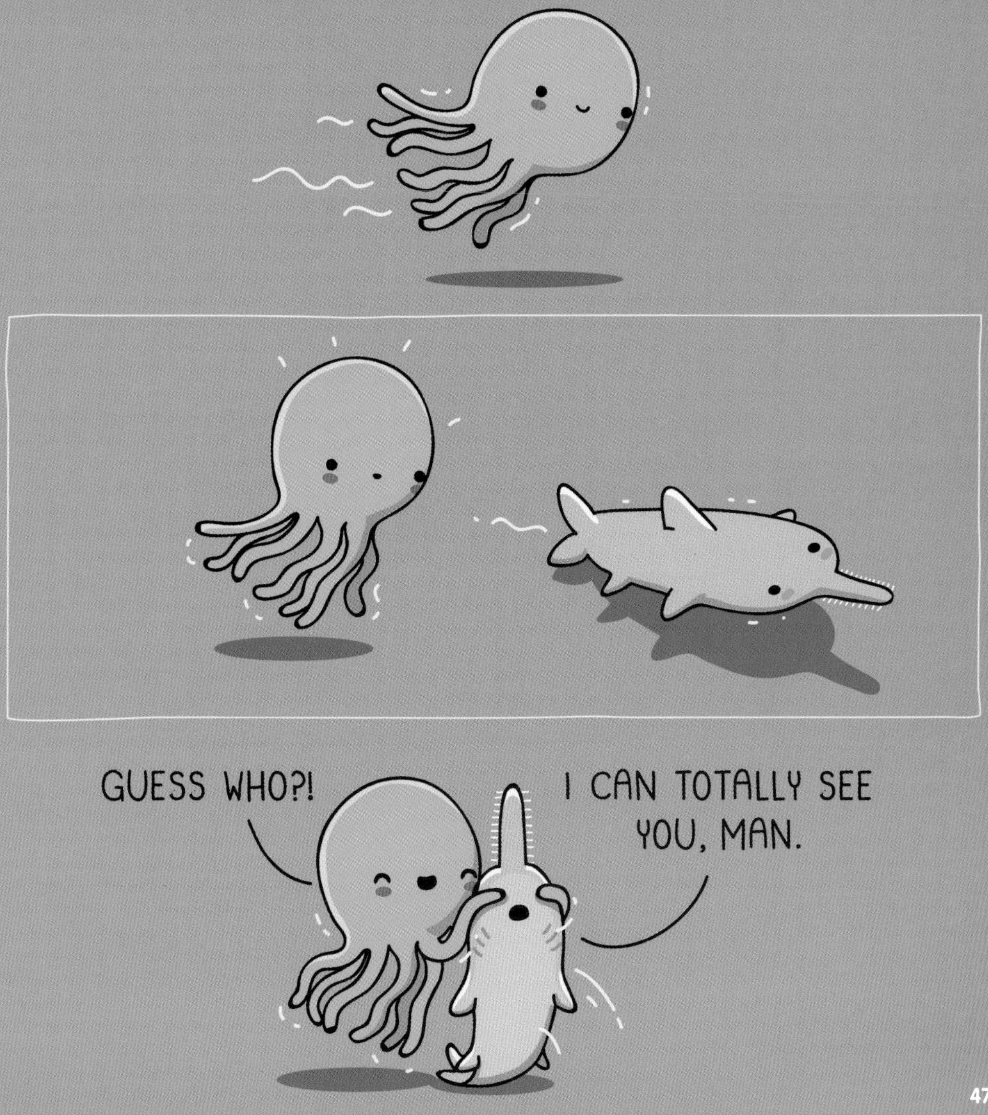
GUESS WHO?!
I CAN TOTALLY SEE YOU, MAN.

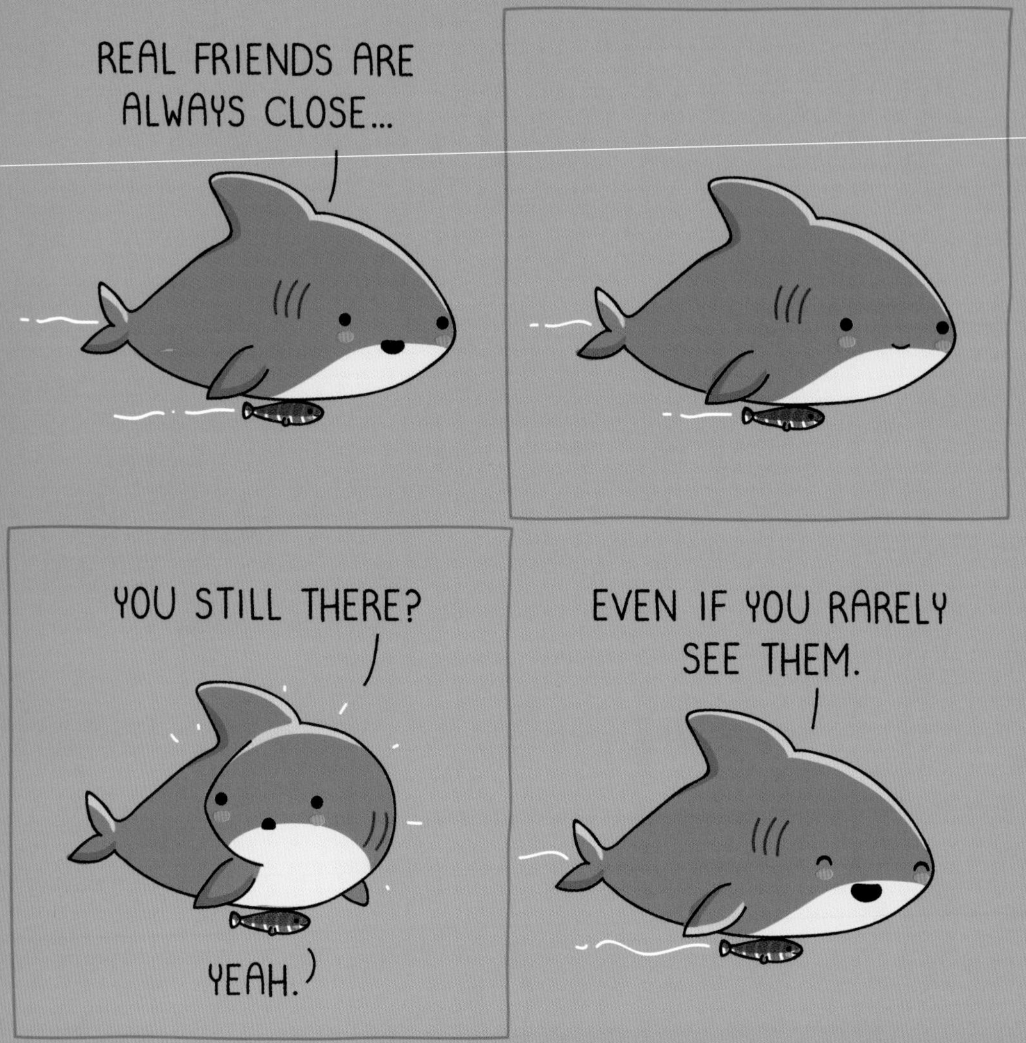
REAL FRIENDS ARE ALWAYS CLOSE...
YOU STILL THERE?
YEAH.
EVEN IF YOU RARELY SEE THEM.

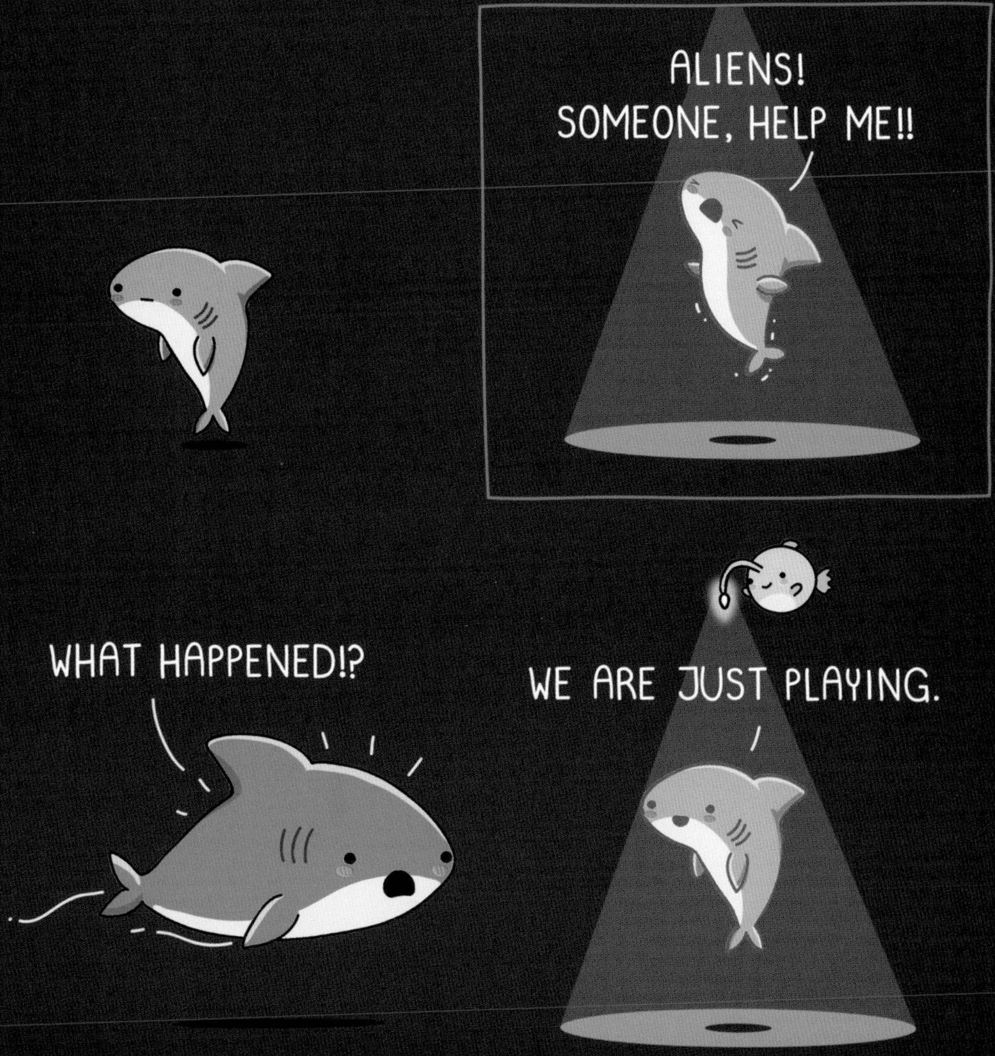
ALIENS!
SOMEONE, HELP ME!!
WHAT HAPPENED!?
WE ARE JUST PLAYING.

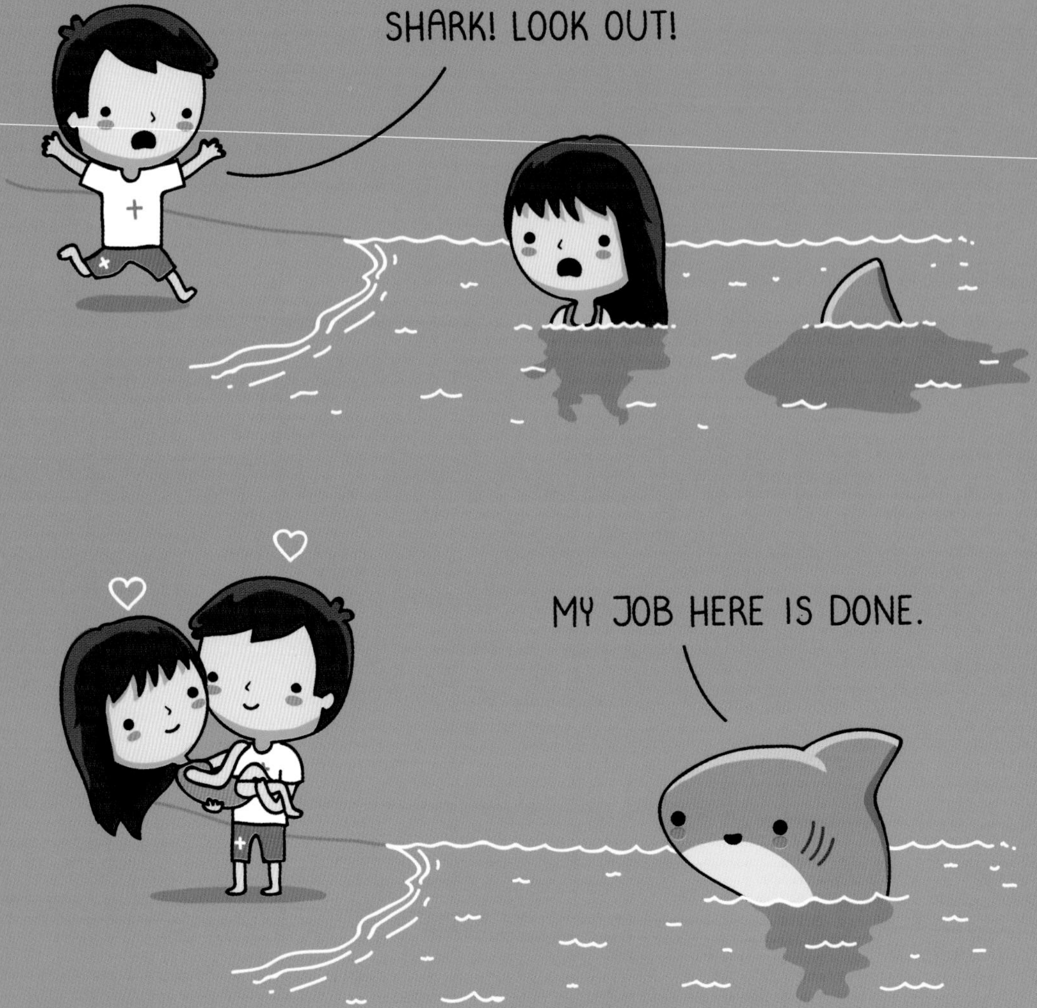
SHARK! LOOK OUT!
MY JOB HERE IS DONE.

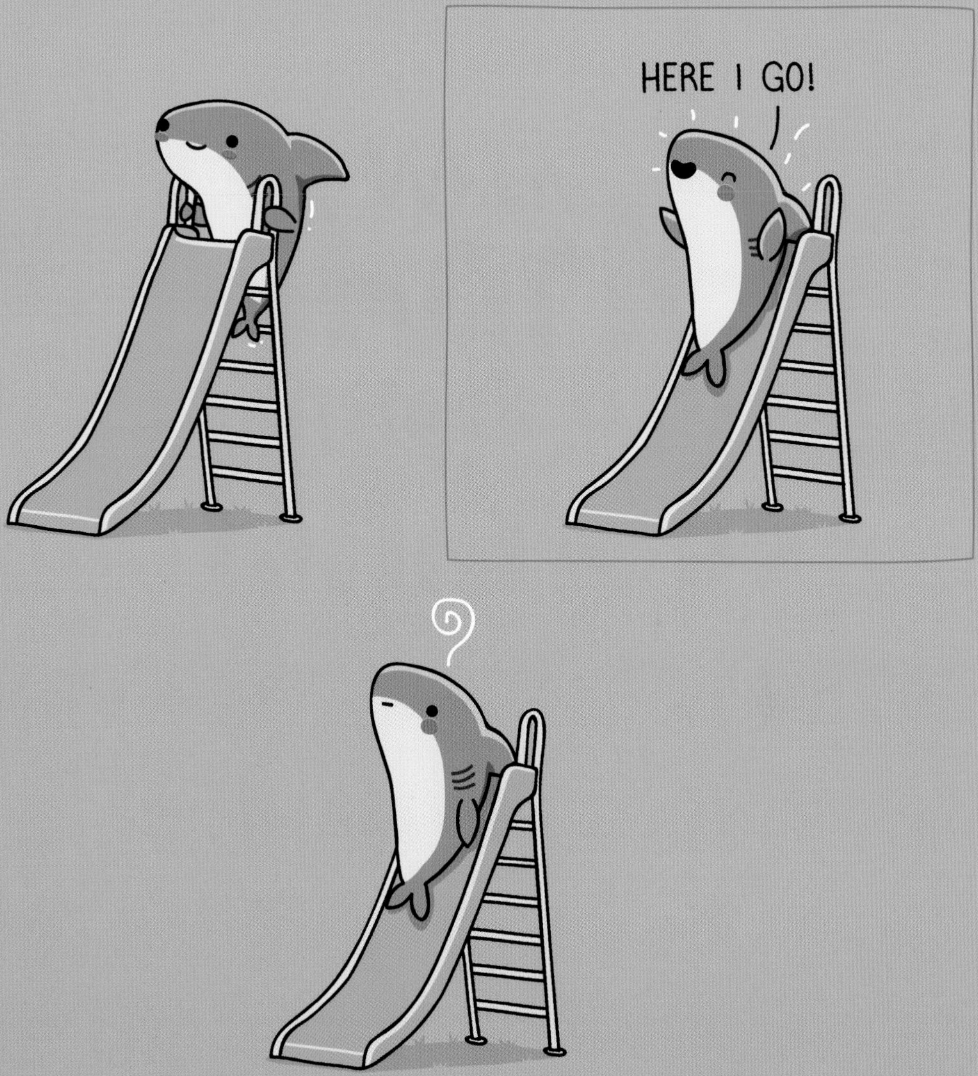
HERE I GO!

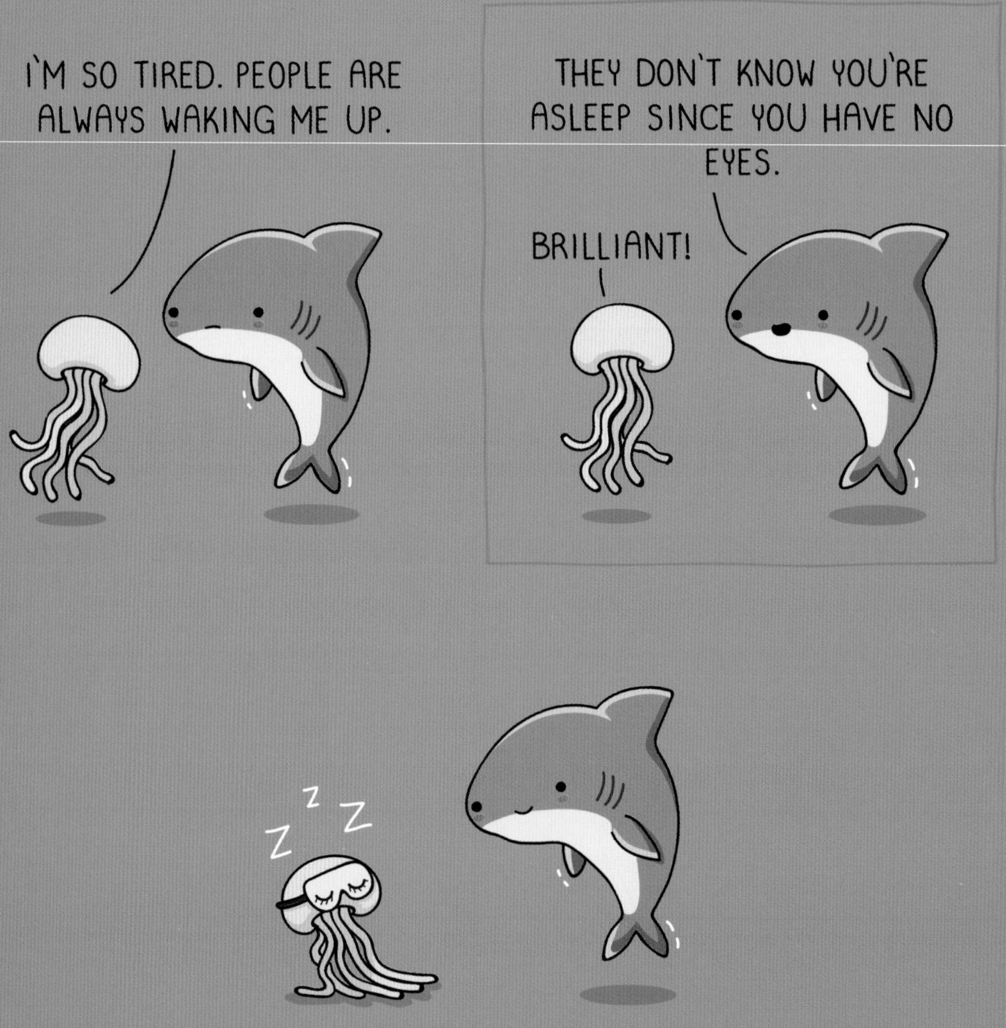
I'M SO TIRED. PEOPLE ARE ALWAYS WAKING ME UP.
THEY DON'T KNOW YOU'RE ASLEEP SINCE YOU HAVE NO EYES.
BRILLIANT!
Z Z Z

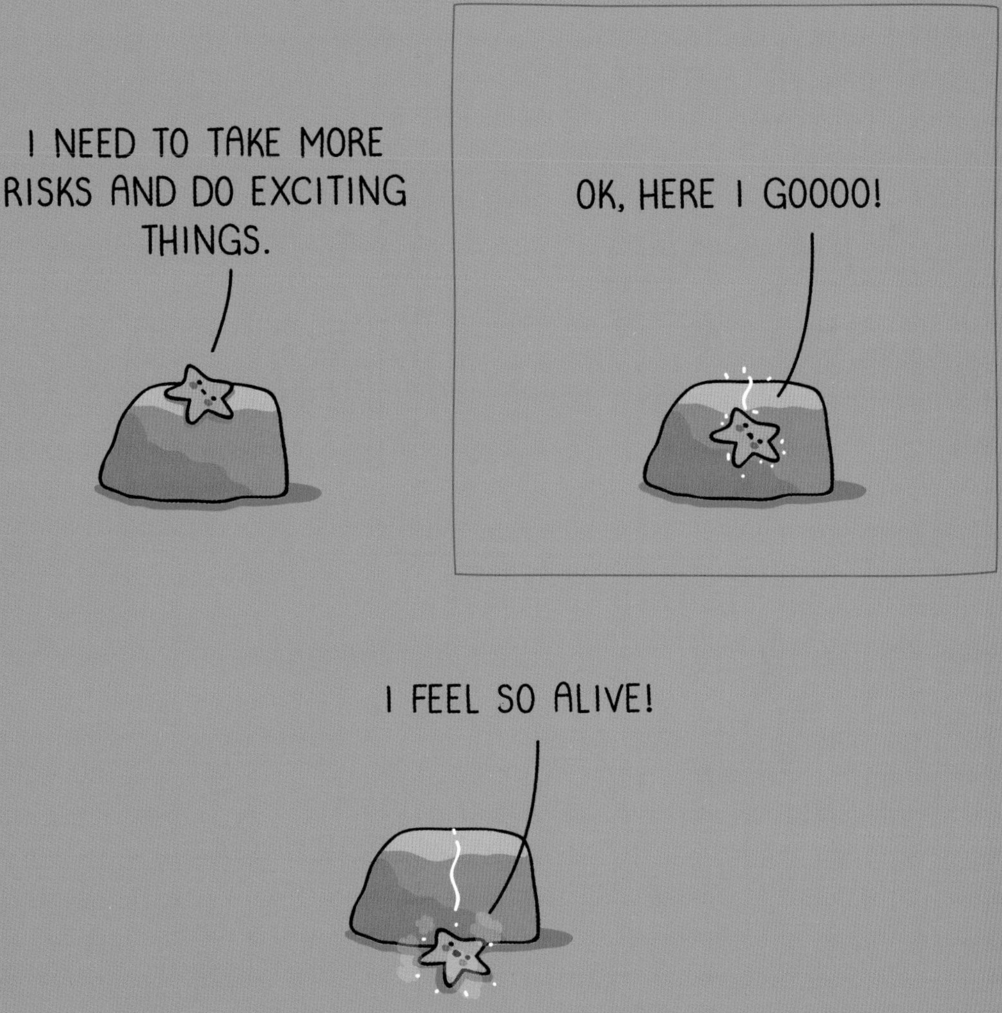
I NEED TO TAKE MORE RISKS AND DO EXCITING THINGS.
OK, HERE I GOOOO!
I FEEL SO ALIVE!

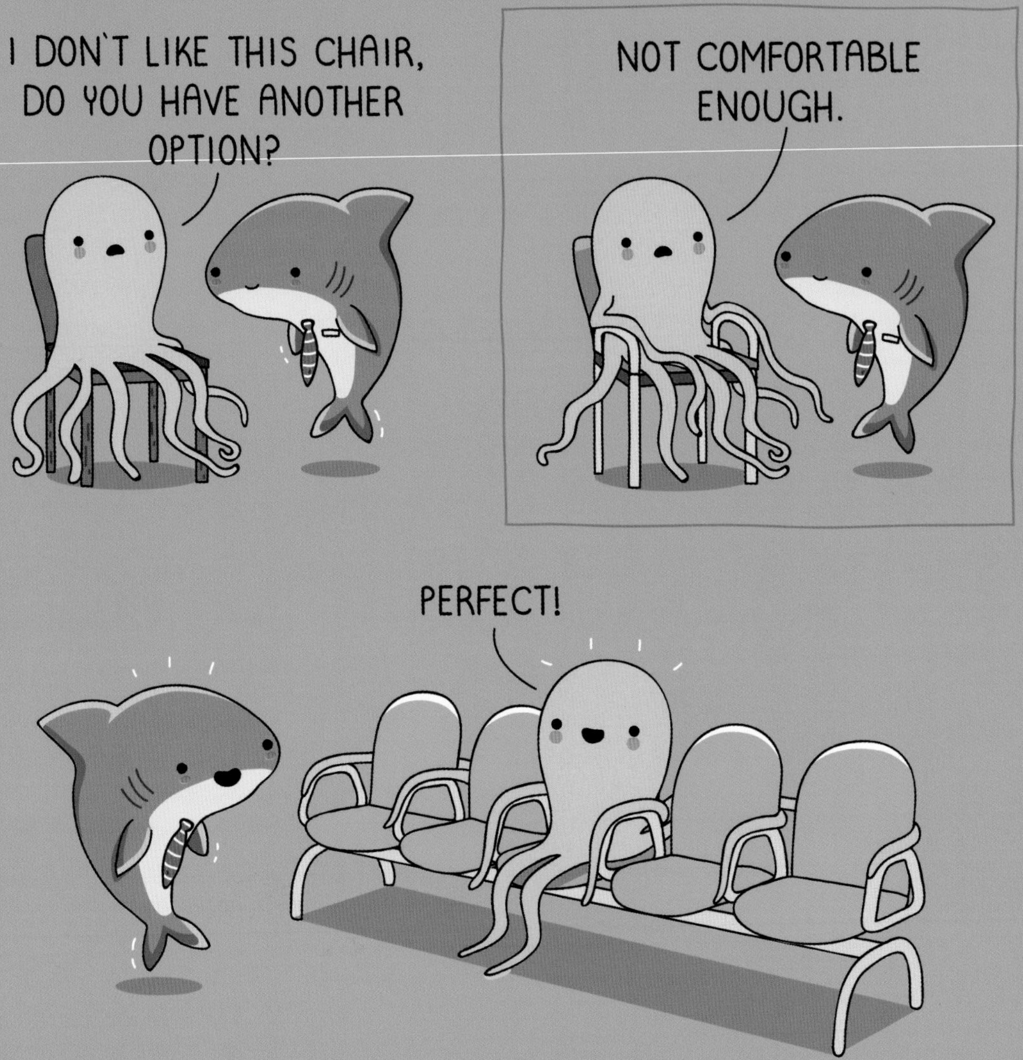
I DON'T LIKE THIS CHAIR, DO YOU HAVE ANOTHER OPTION?
NOT COMFORTABLE ENOUGH.
PERFECT!

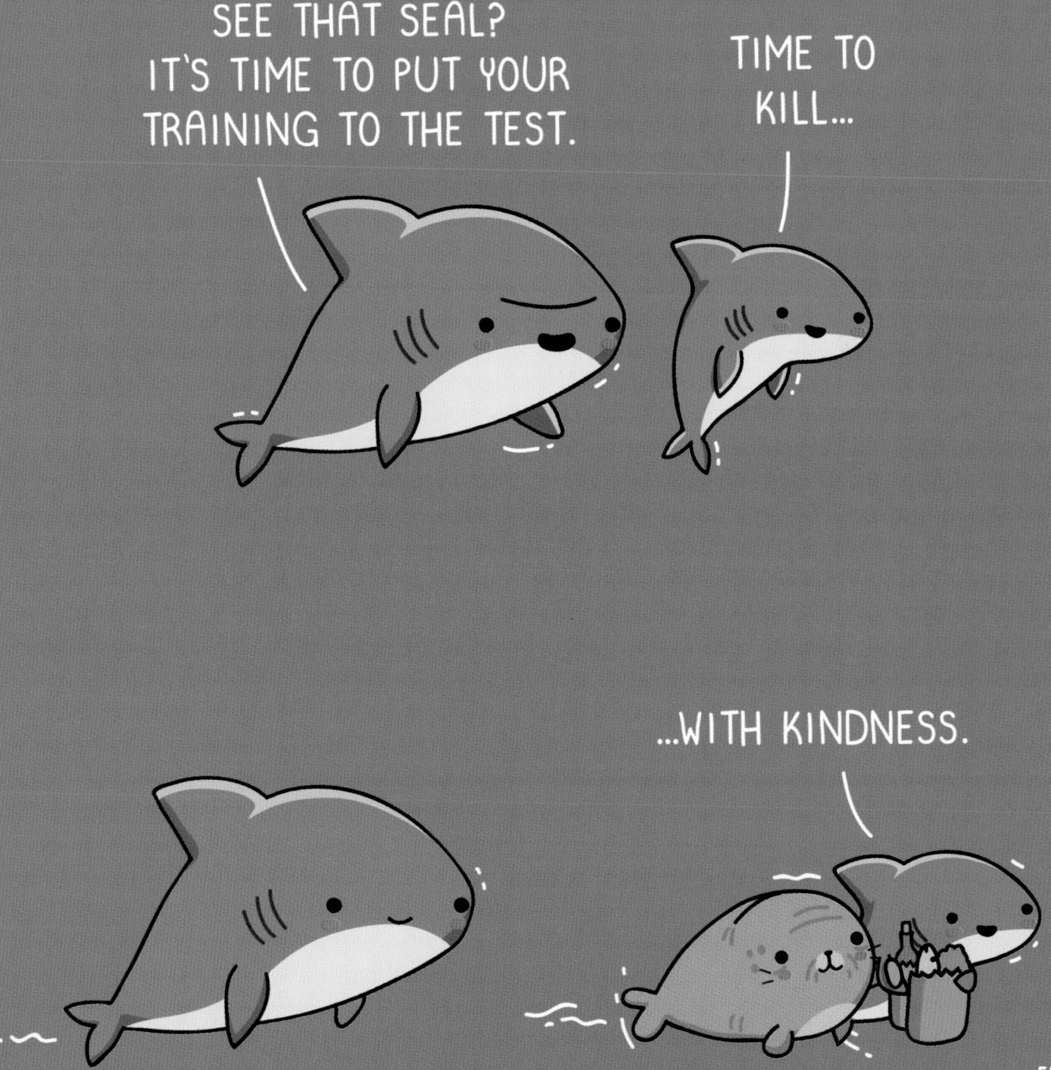
SEE THAT SEAL?
IT'S TIME TO PUT YOUR TRAINING TO THE TEST.
TIME TO KILL...
...WITH KINDNESS.

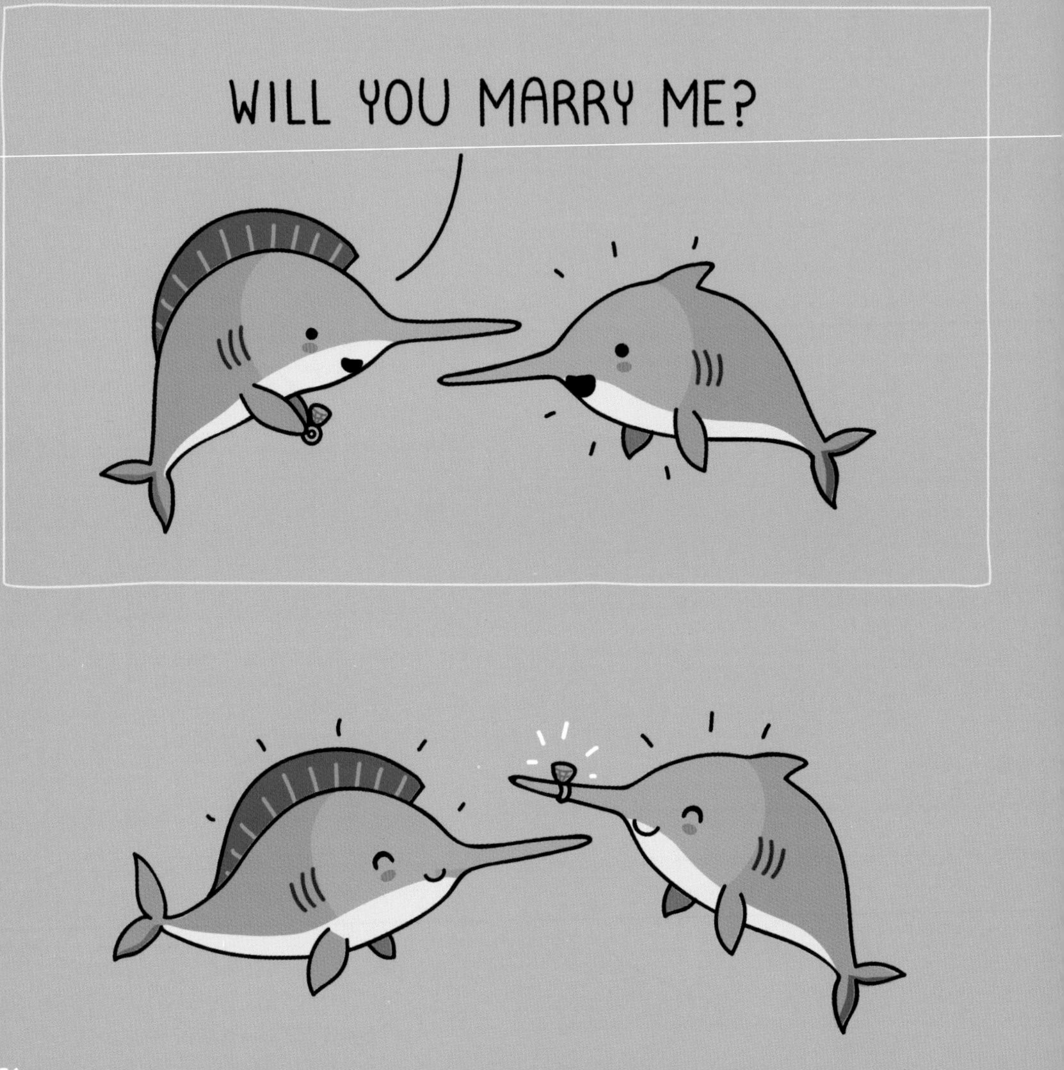
WILL YOU MARRY ME?

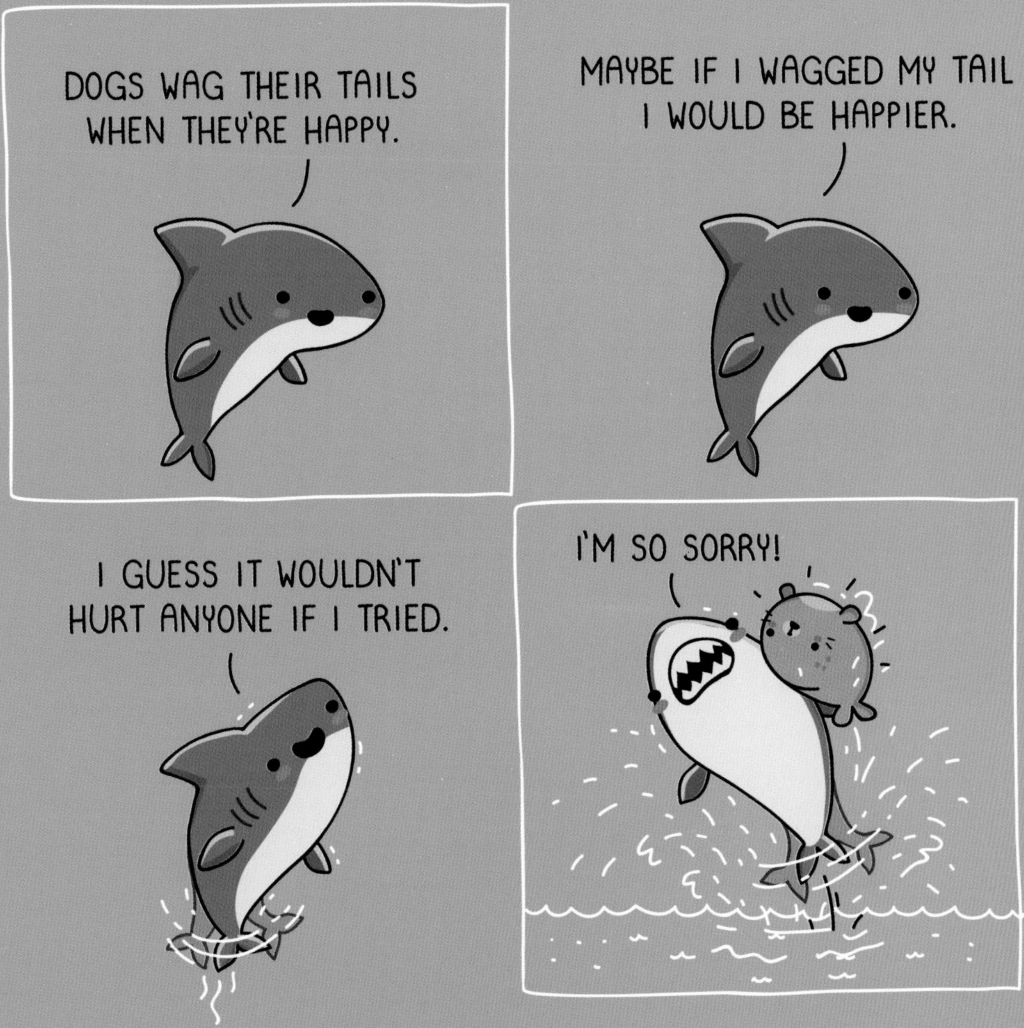
DOGS WAG THEIR TAILS WHEN THEY'RE HAPPY.
MAYBE IF I WAGGED MY TAIL I WOULD BE HAPPIER.
I GUESS IT WOULDN'T HURT ANYONE IF I TRIED.
I'M SO SORRY!

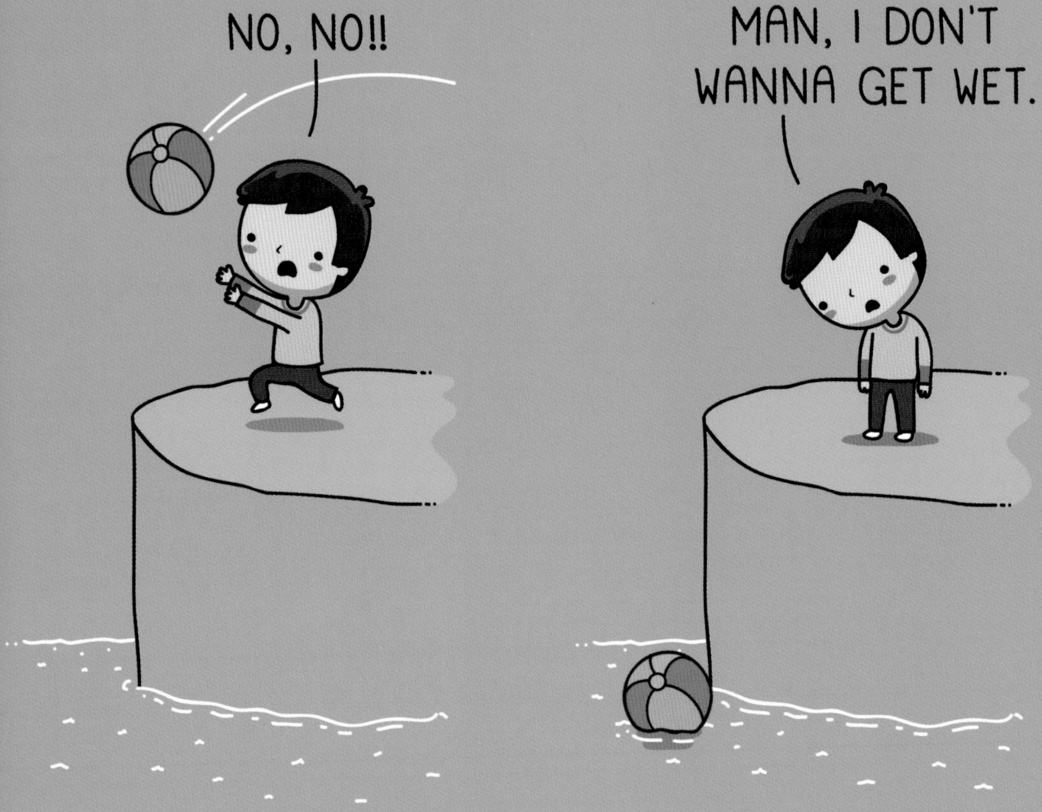
NO, NO!!
MAN, I DON'T WANNA GET WET.

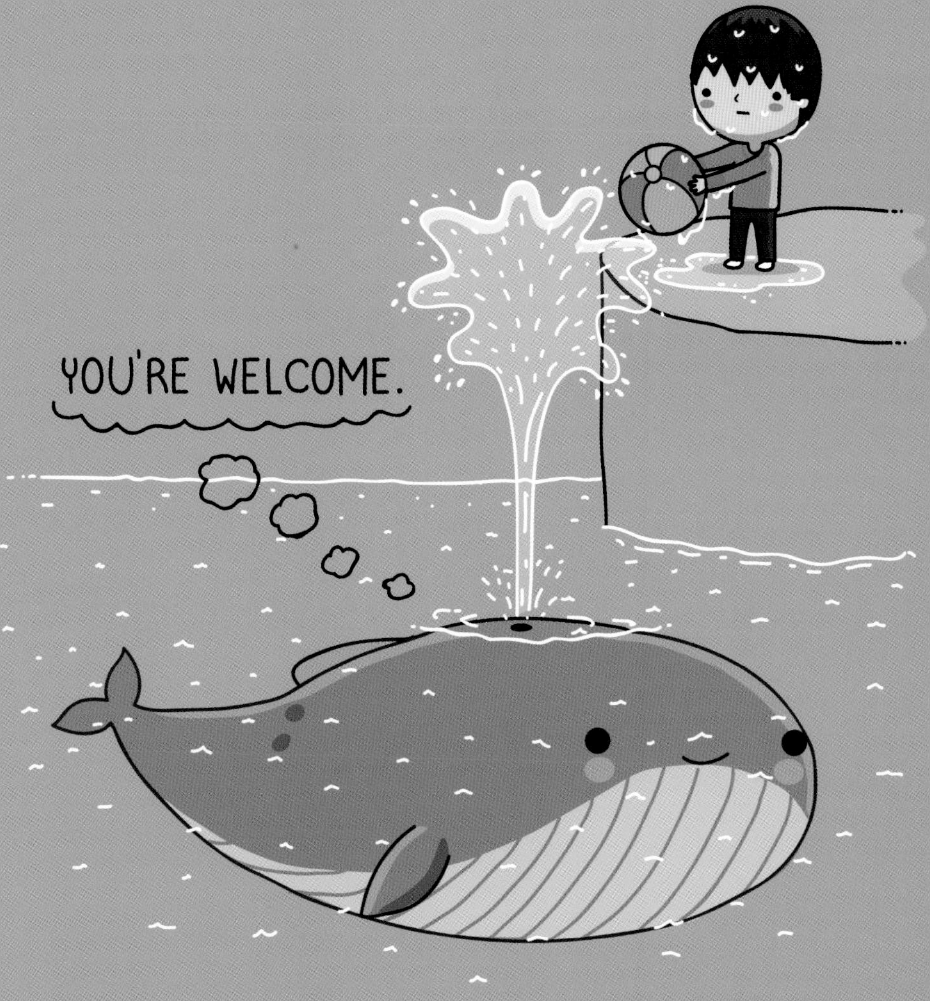
YOU'RE WELCOME.

AFTER ALL THIS TIME
SEARCHING,
WE FINALLY FOUND ONE.

WHERE THERE'S A WILL...

THERE'S A WHALE.

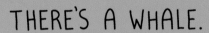

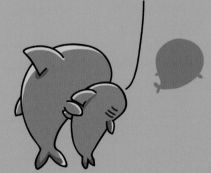

60

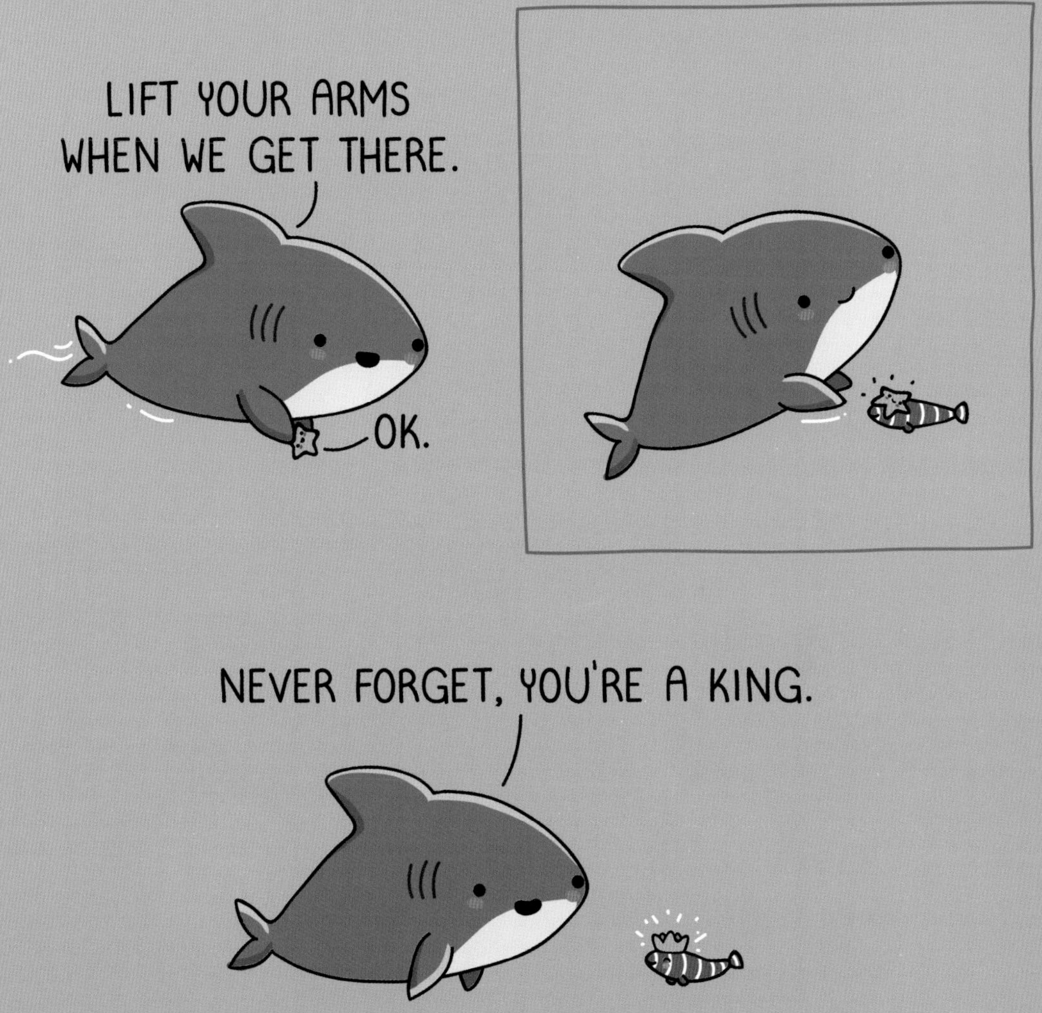
LIFT YOUR ARMS WHEN WE GET THERE.
OK.
NEVER FORGET, YOU'RE A KING.

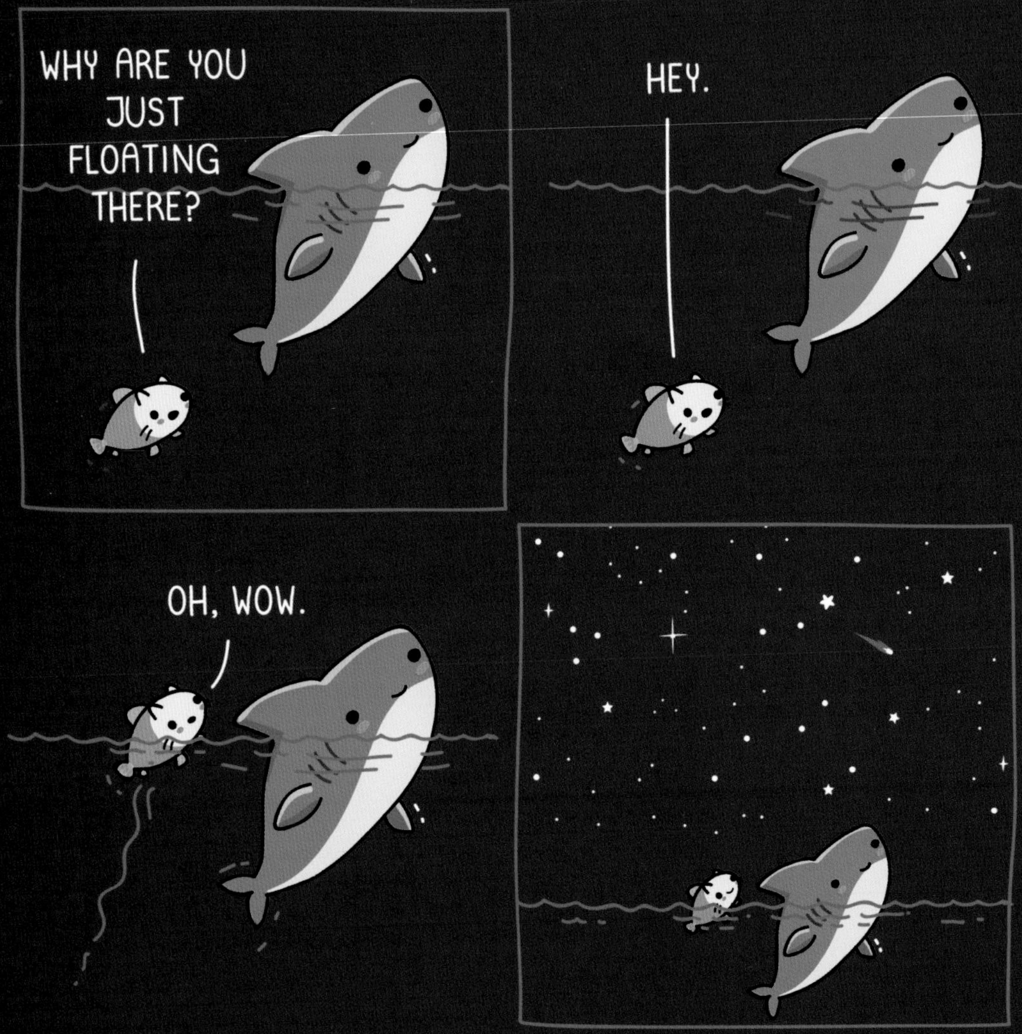
WHY ARE YOU JUST FLOATING THERE?
HEY.
OH, WOW.

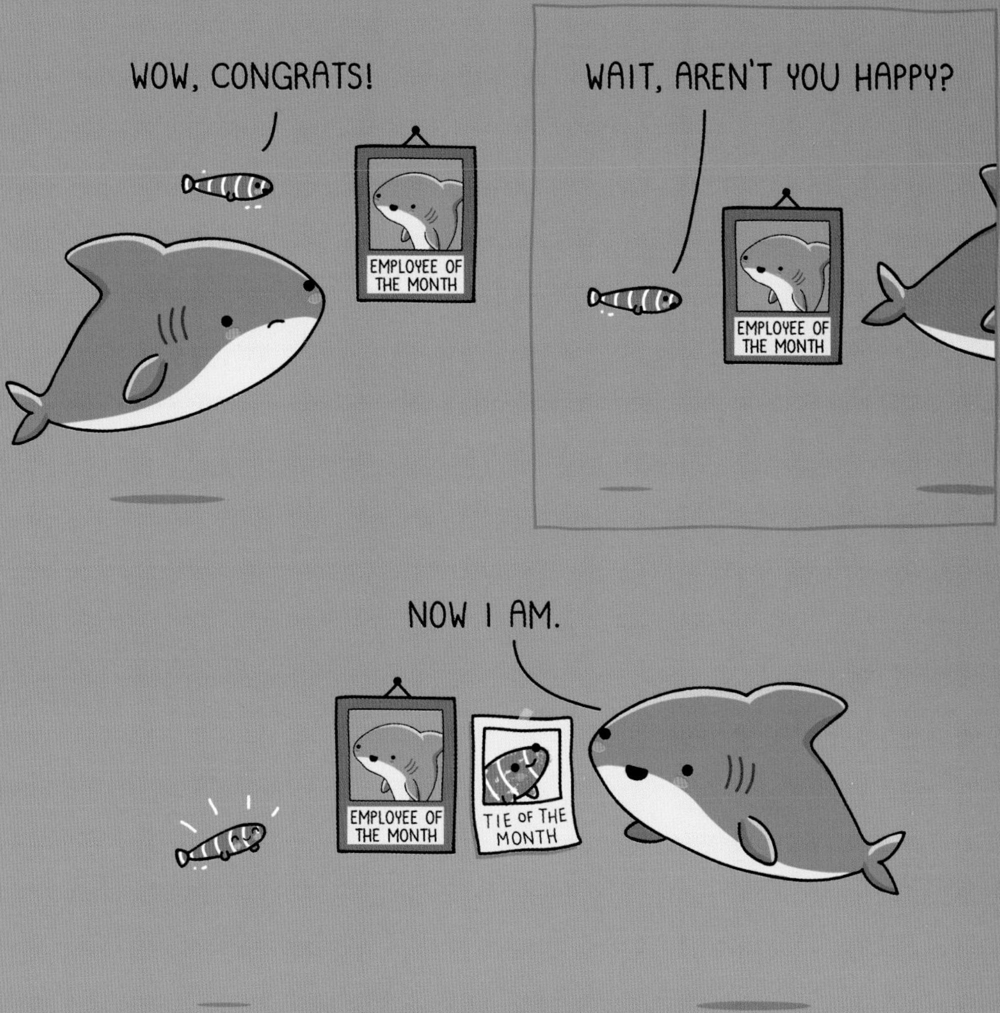
WOW, CONGRATS!
EMPLOYEE OF THE MONTH
WAIT, AREN'T YOU HAPPY?
EMPLOYEE OF THE MONTH
NOW I AM.
EMPLOYEE OF THE MONTH
TIE OF THE MONTH

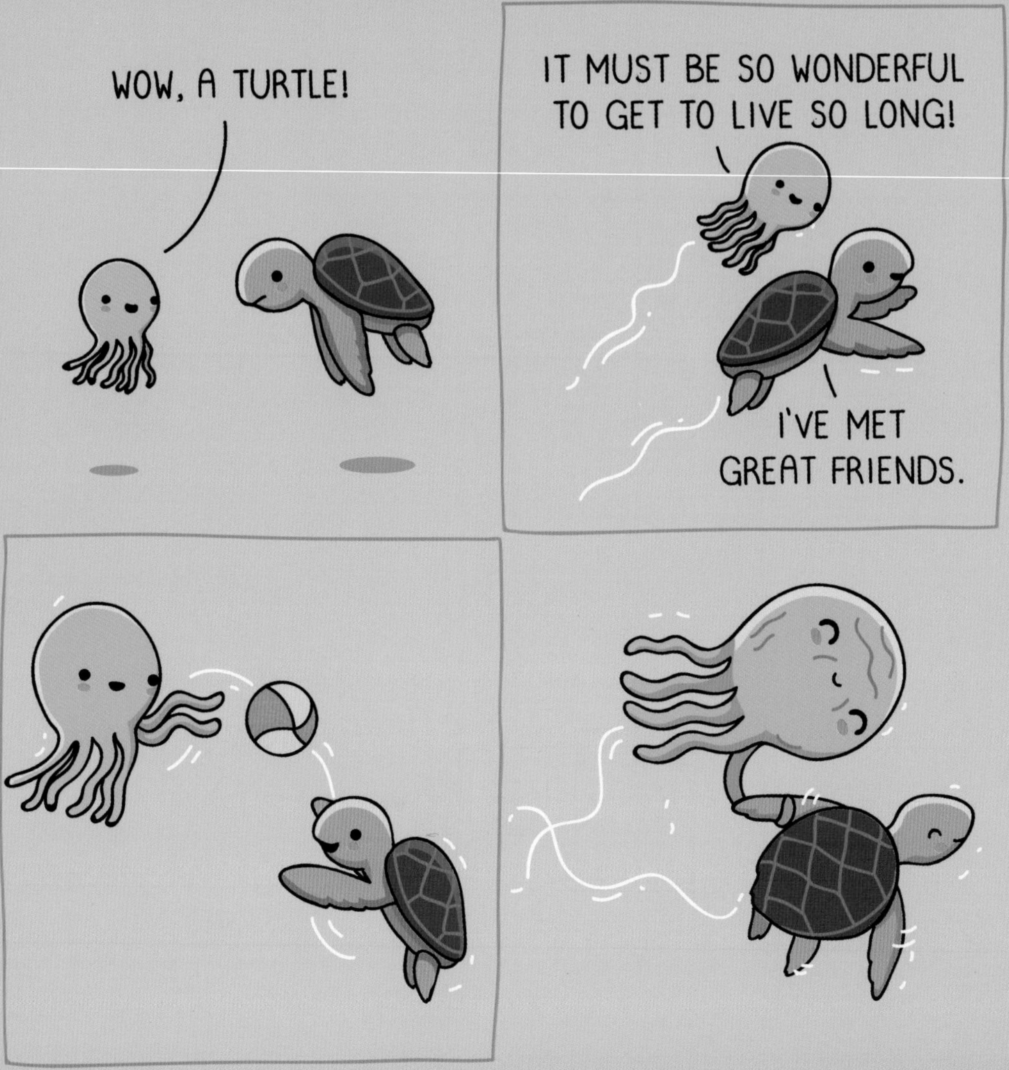
WOW, A TURTLE!
IT MUST BE SO WONDERFUL TO GET TO LIVE SO LONG!
I'VE MET GREAT FRIENDS.

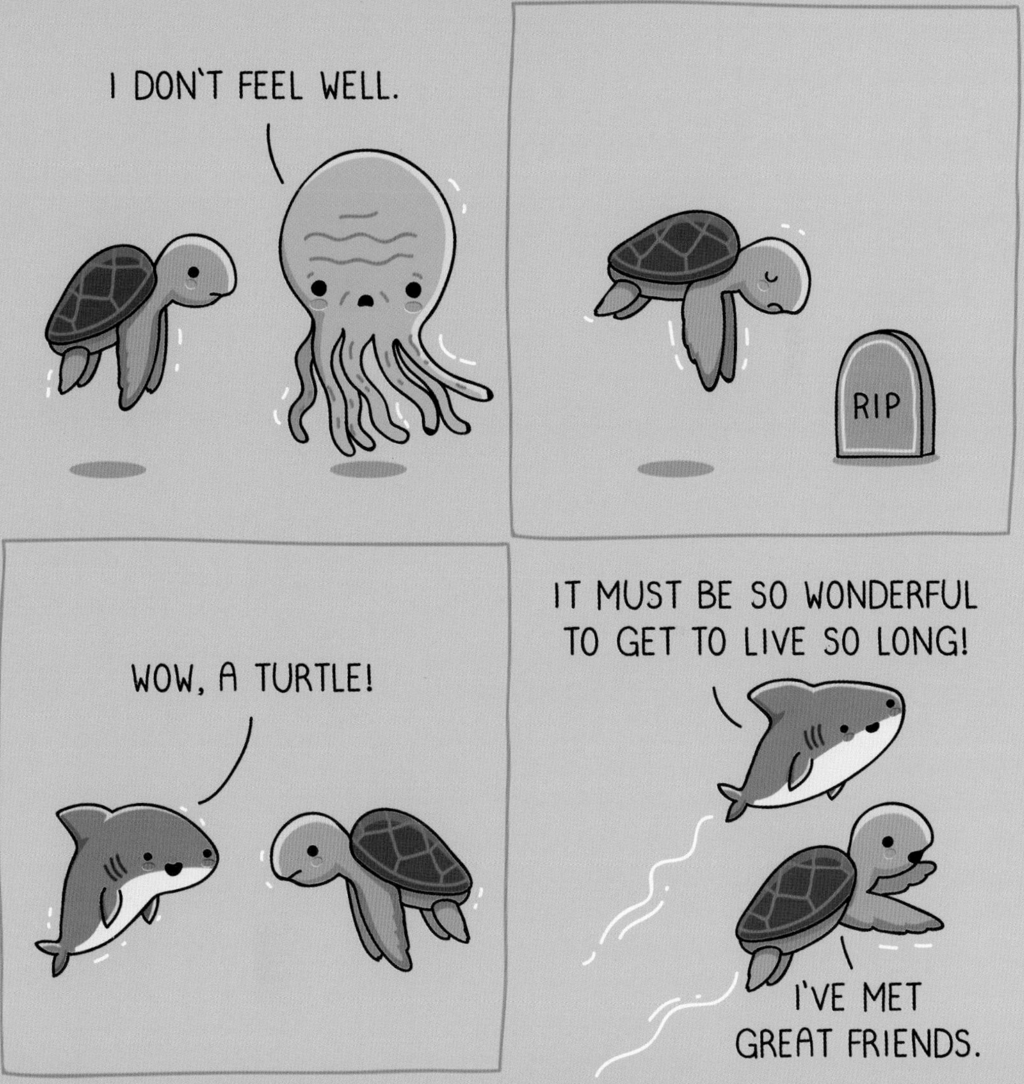
I DON'T FEEL WELL.
RIP
WOW, A TURTLE!
IT MUST BE SO WONDERFUL TO GET TO LIVE SO LONG!
I'VE MET GREAT FRIENDS.

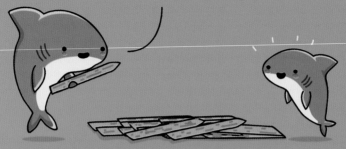

YOU'RE BIG ENOUGH TO HELP ME BUILD THE FENCE.

BRING ME A HAMMER.

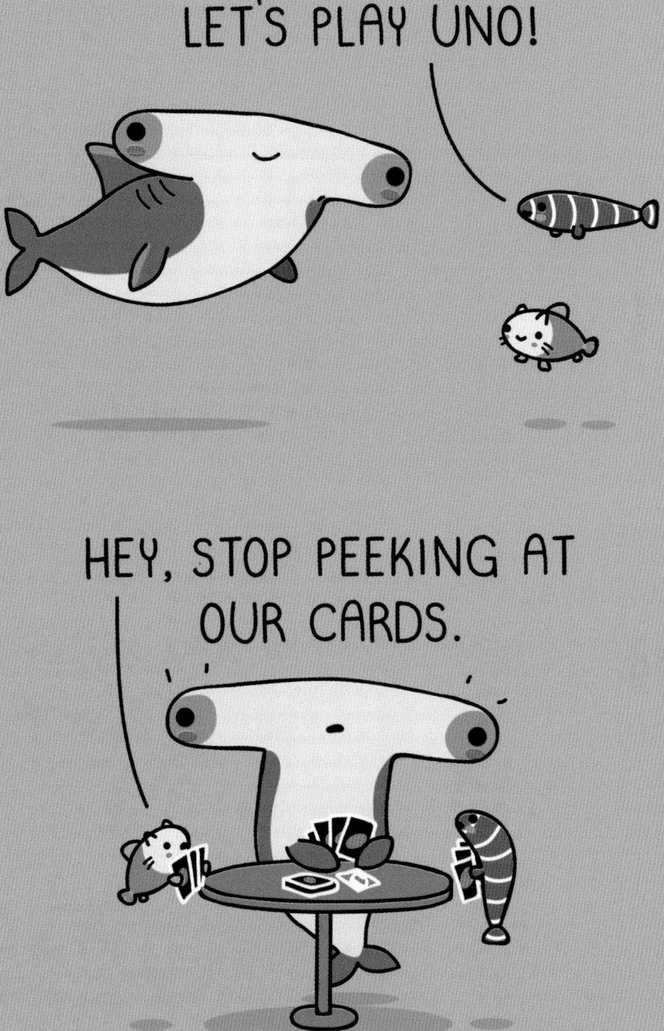
LET'S PLAY UNO!
HEY, STOP PEEKING AT OUR CARDS.

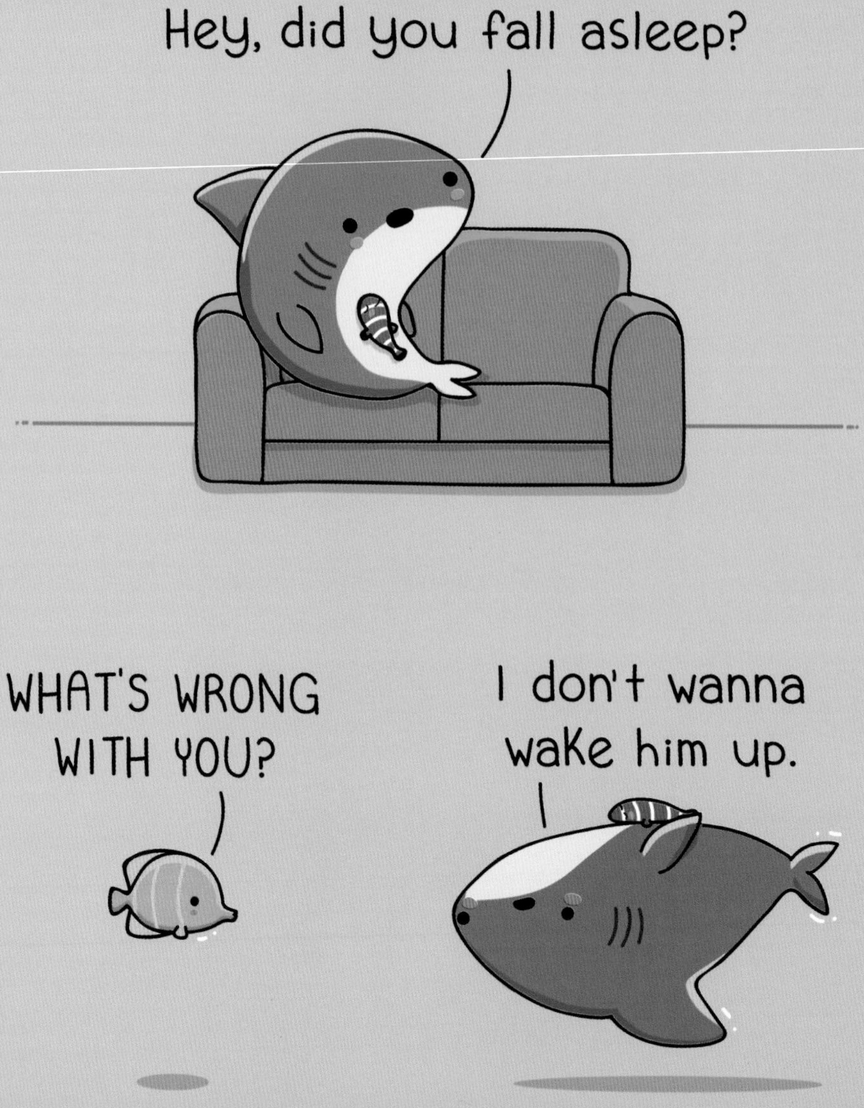
Hey, did you fall asleep?
WHAT'S WRONG WITH YOU?
I don't wanna wake him up.

SOMETIMES IT MIGHT FEEL LIKE IT...

BUT YOU'RE NEVER ALONE.

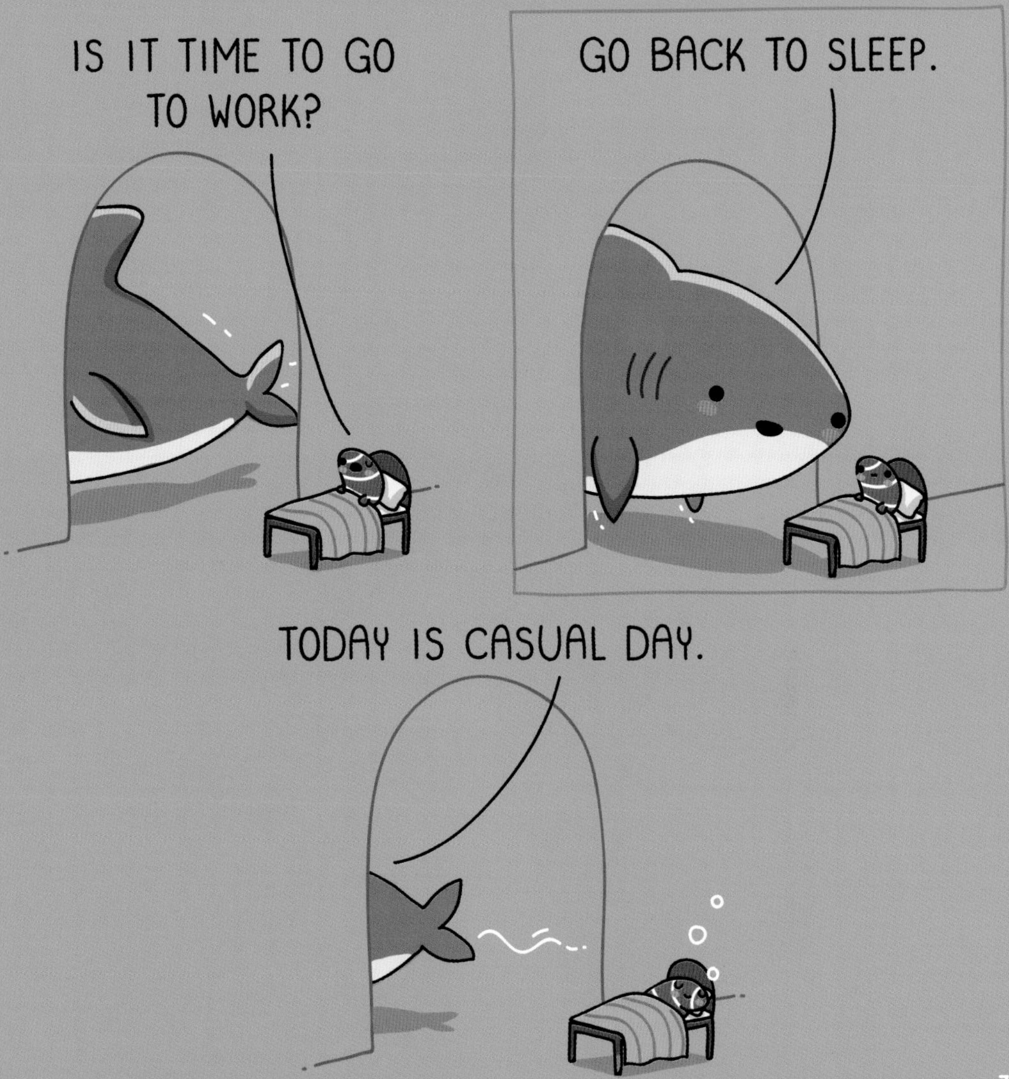
IS IT TIME TO GO TO WORK?
GO BACK TO SLEEP.
TODAY IS CASUAL DAY.

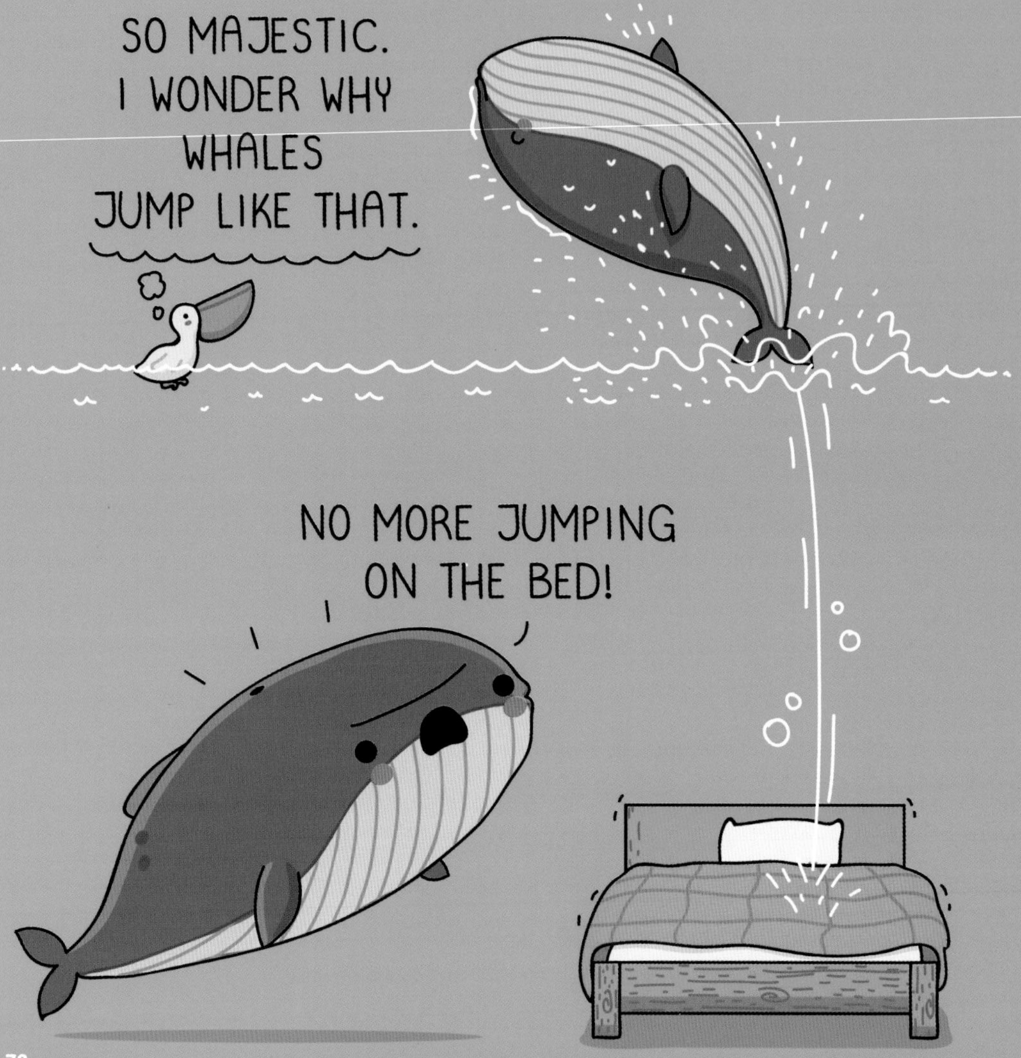
SO MAJESTIC. I WONDER WHY WHALES JUMP LIKE THAT.
NO MORE JUMPING ON THE BED!

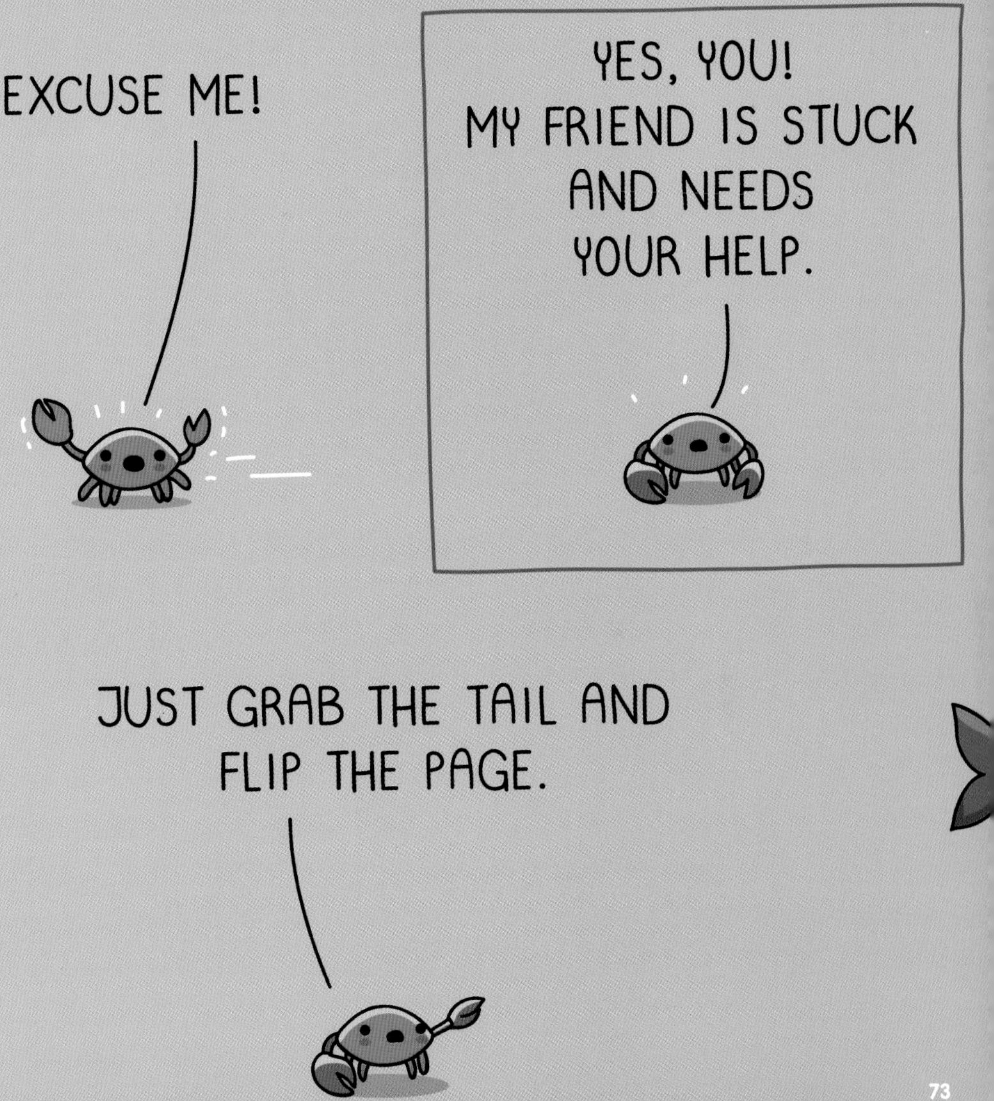
EXCUSE ME!
YES, YOU!
MY FRIEND IS STUCK
AND NEEDS
YOUR HELP.
JUST GRAB THE TAIL AND
FLIP THE PAGE.

THANK YOU SO MUCH, KIND STRANGER!
I WON'T SWING SO HARD NEXT TIME.

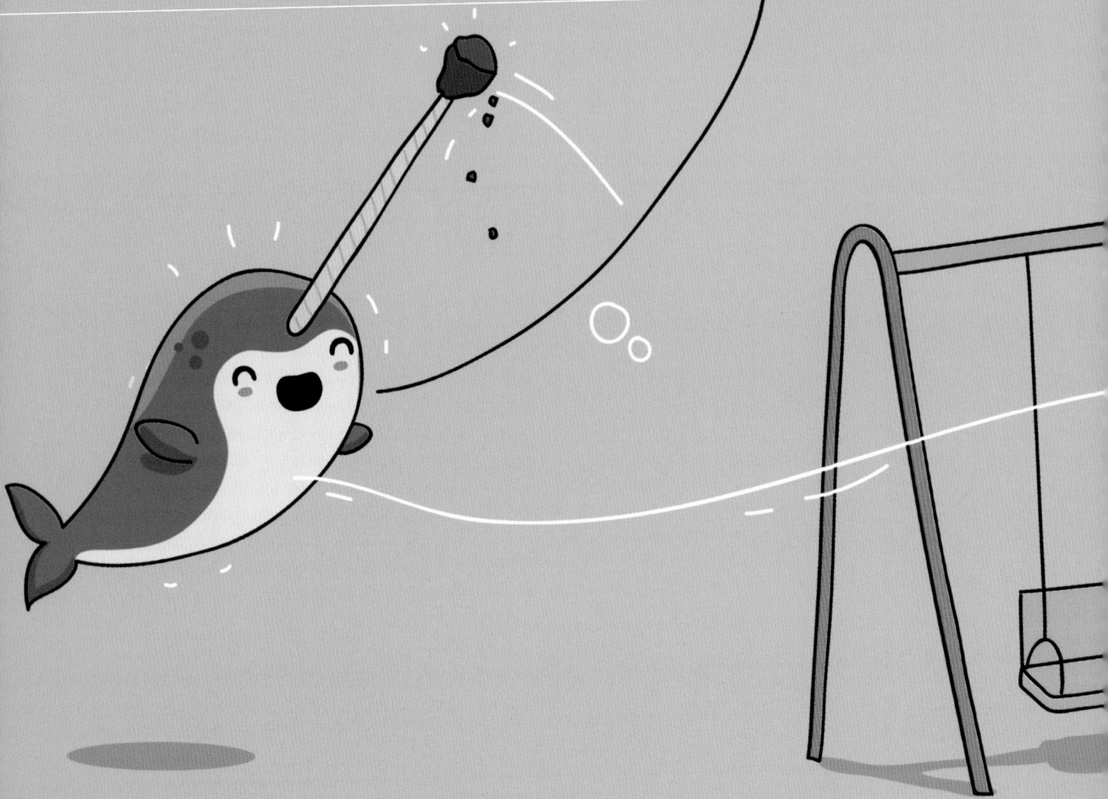

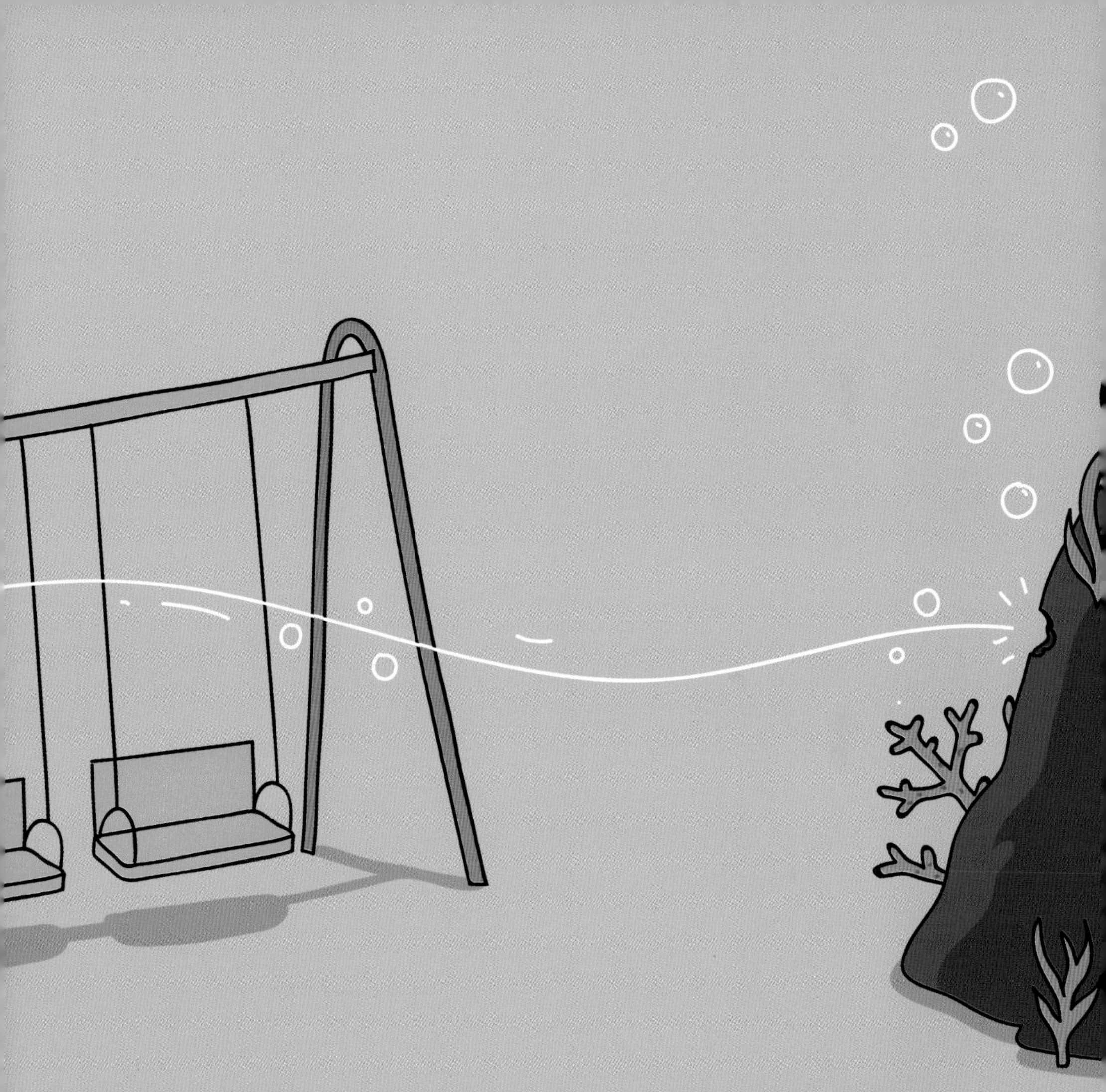

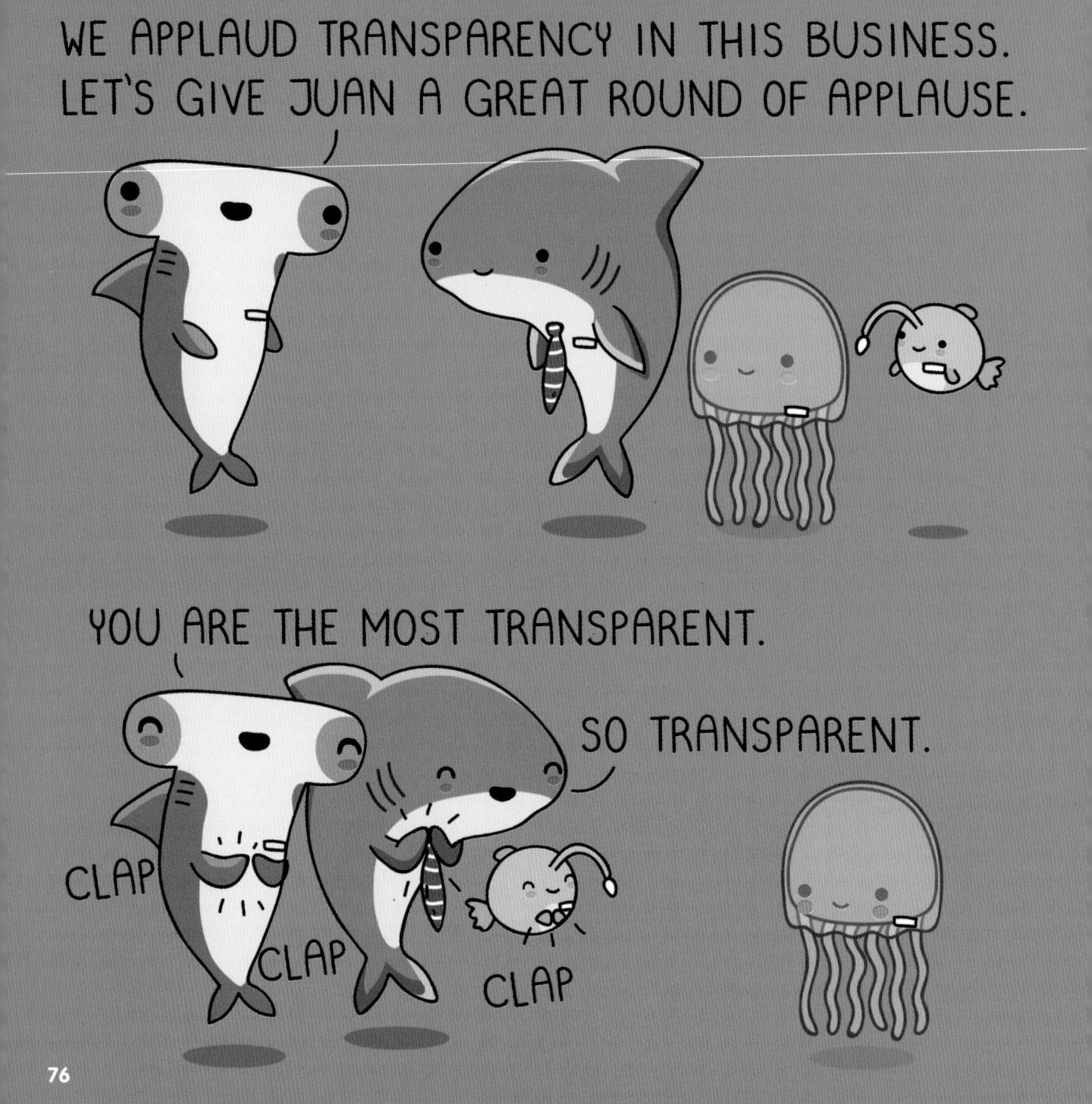
WE APPLAUD TRANSPARENCY IN THIS BUSINESS. LET'S GIVE JUAN A GREAT ROUND OF APPLAUSE.
YOU ARE THE MOST TRANSPARENT.
SO TRANSPARENT.
CLAP
CLAP
CLAP

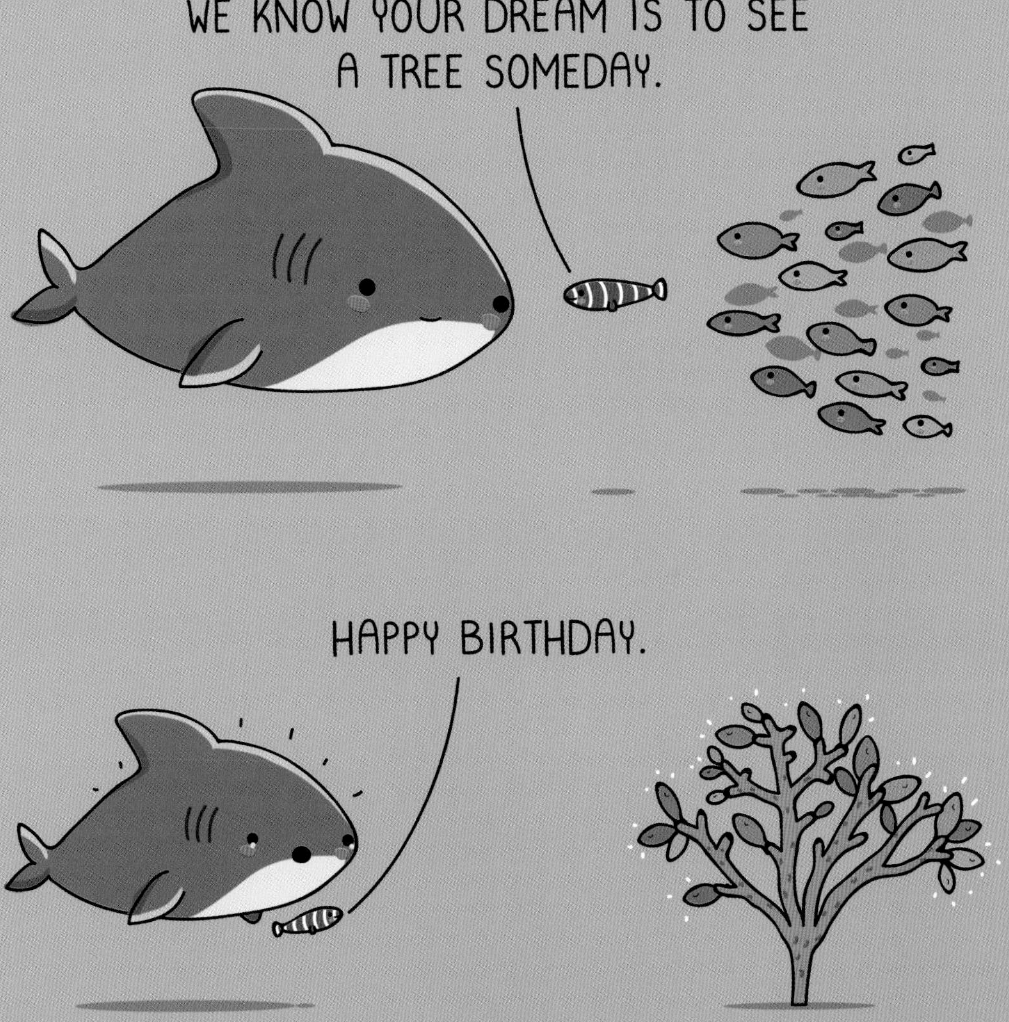
WE KNOW YOUR DREAM IS TO SEE A TREE SOMEDAY.
HAPPY BIRTHDAY.

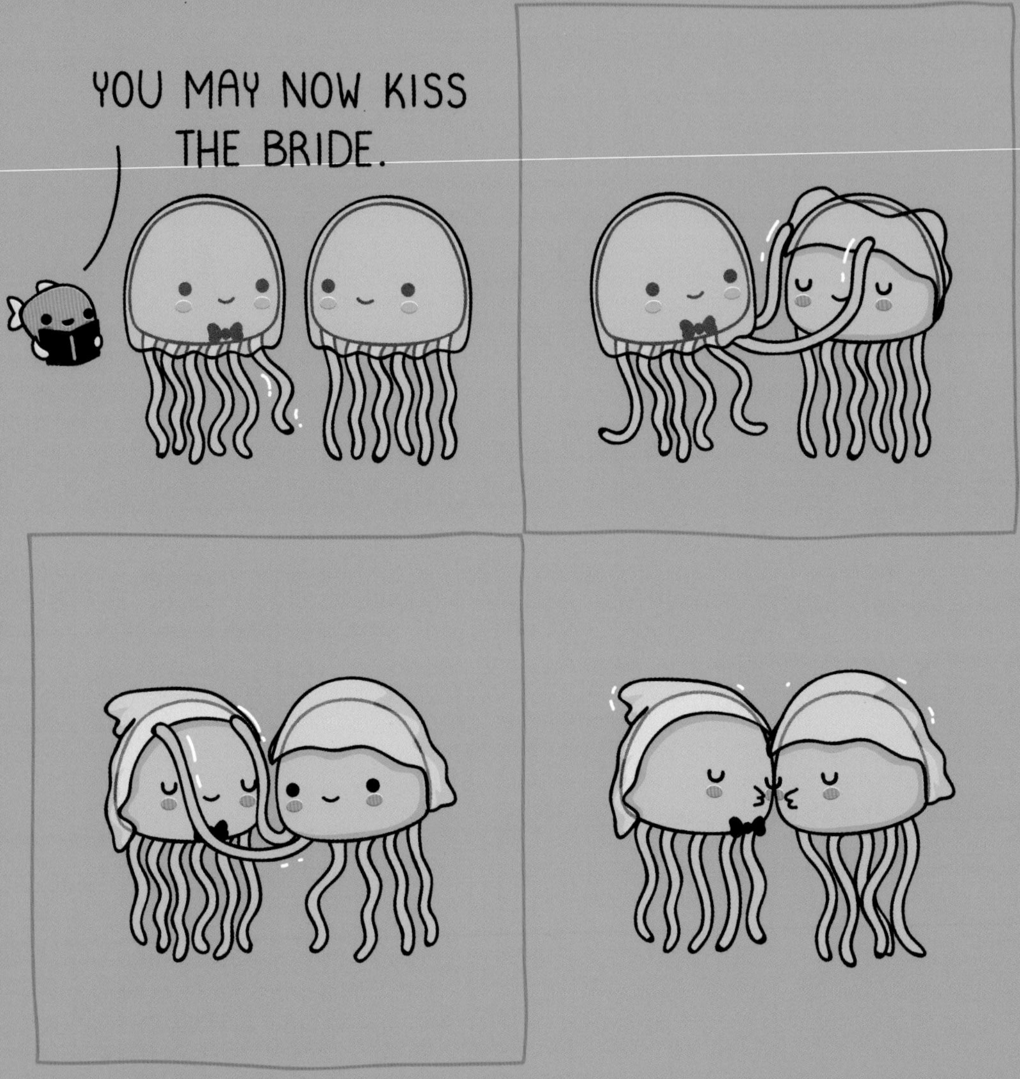
YOU MAY NOW KISS THE BRIDE.

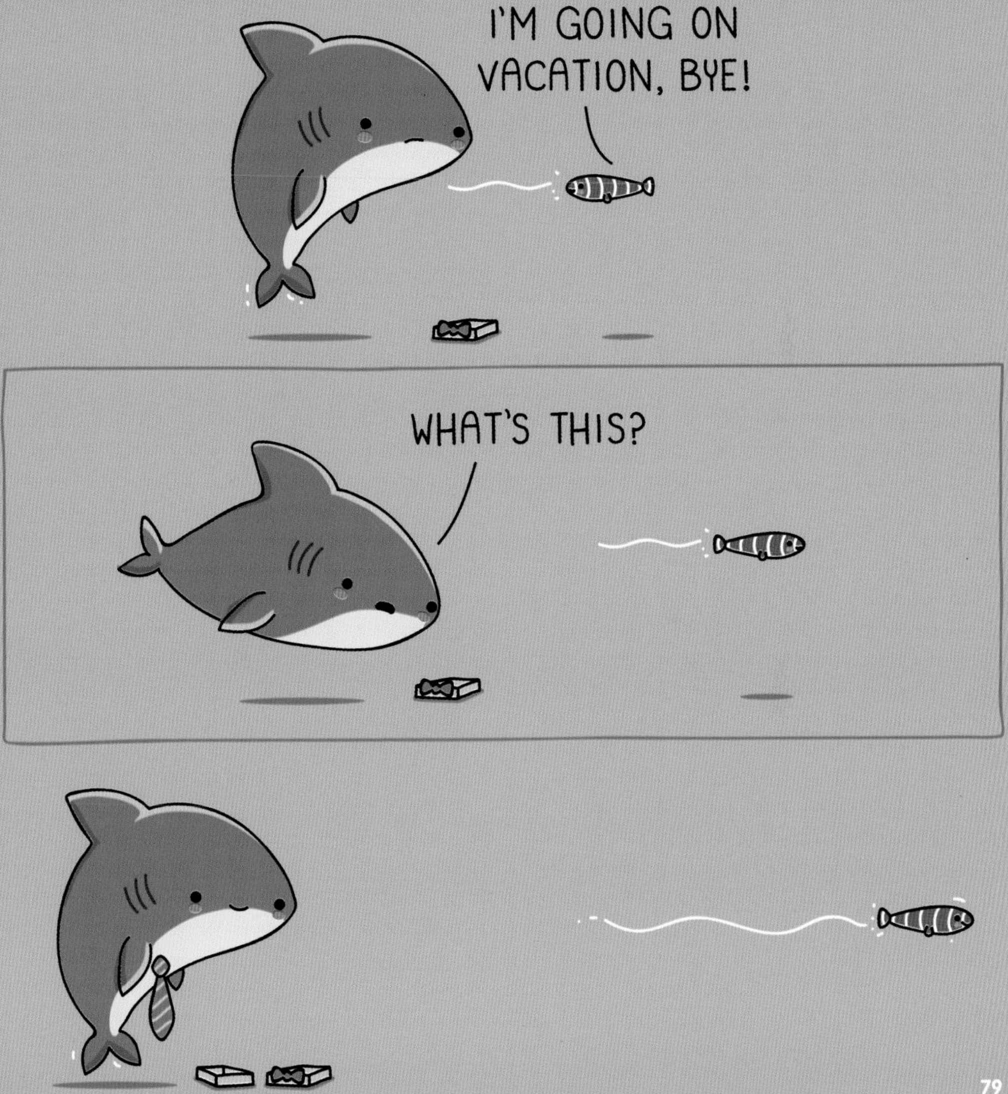
I'M GOING ON VACATION, BYE!
WHAT'S THIS?

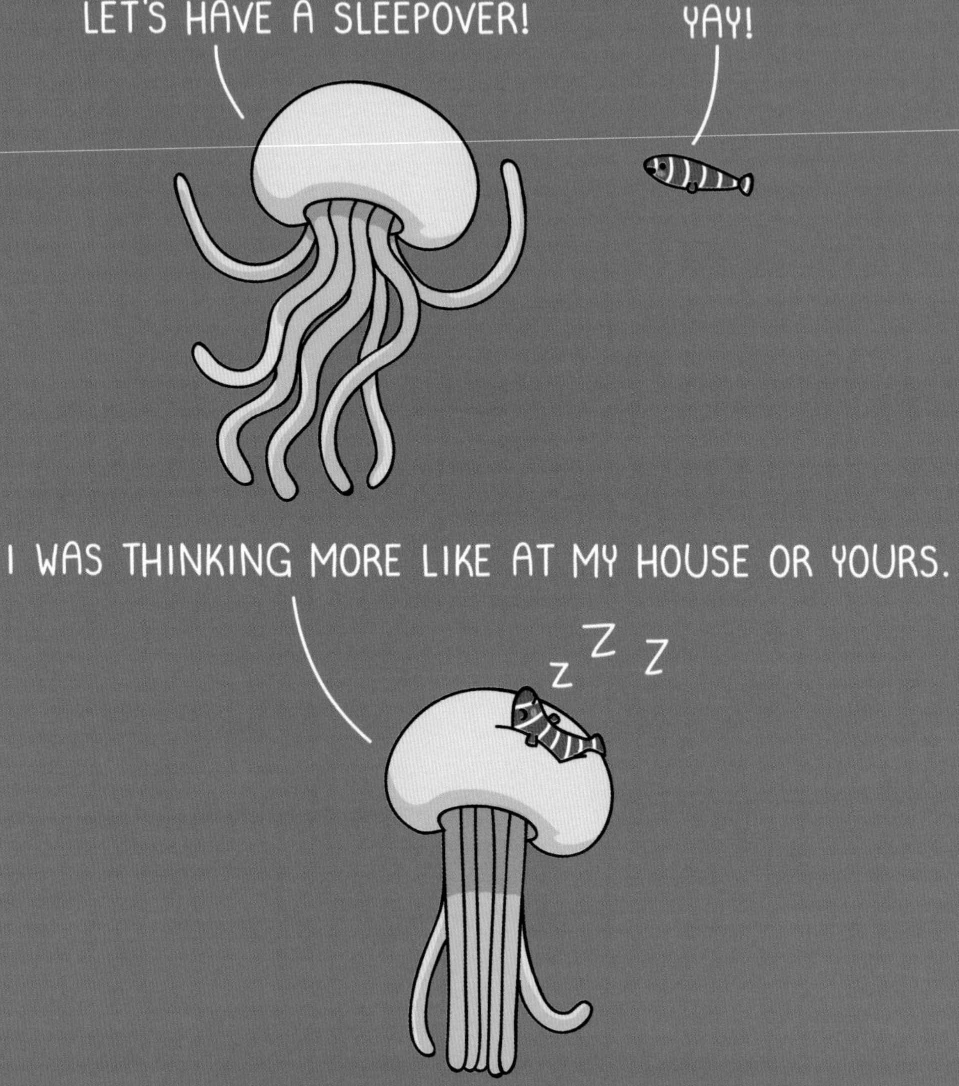
LET'S HAVE A SLEEPOVER!
YAY!
I WAS THINKING MORE LIKE AT MY HOUSE OR YOURS.
Z Z Z

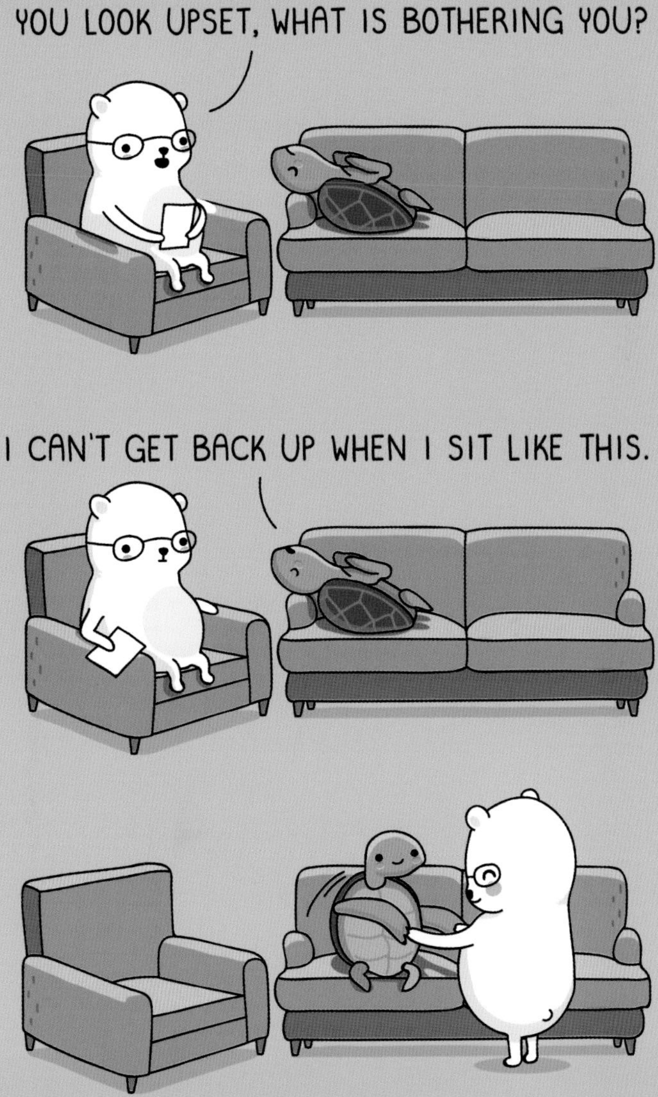
YOU LOOK UPSET, WHAT IS BOTHERING YOU?
I CAN'T GET BACK UP WHEN I SIT LIKE THIS.

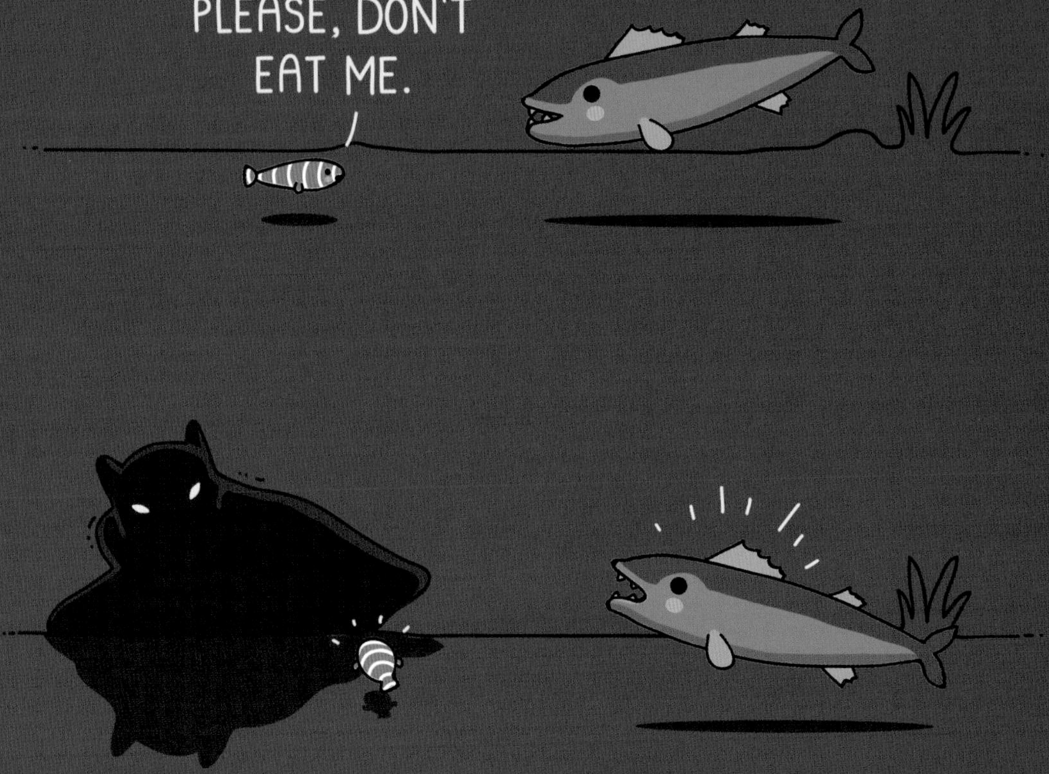
PLEASE, DON'T EAT ME.

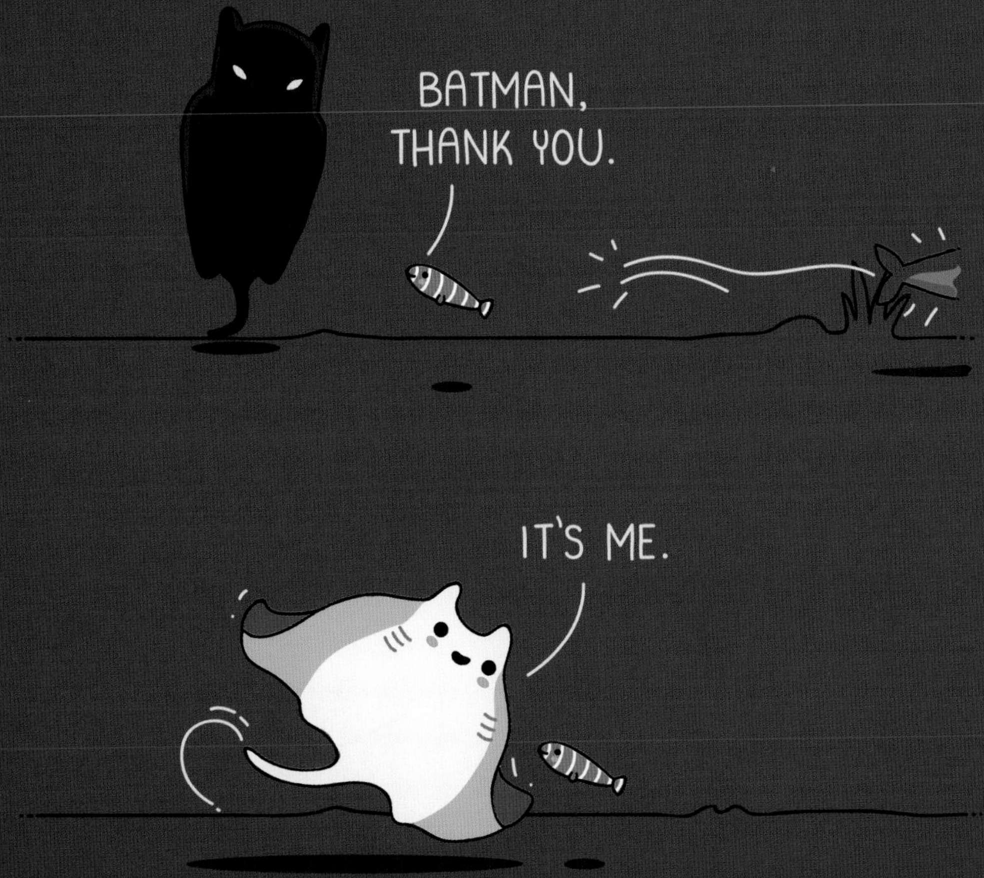
BATMAN,
THANK YOU.
IT'S ME.

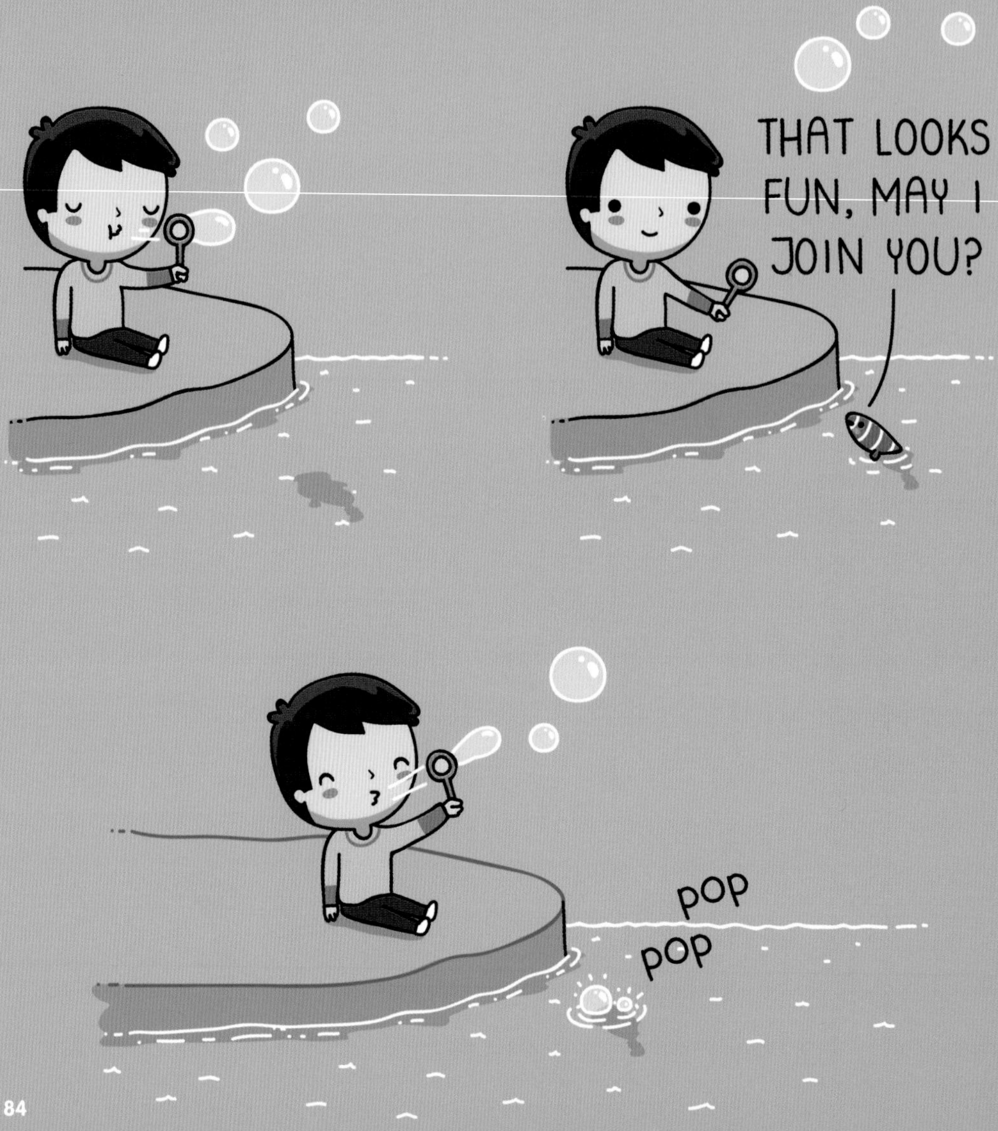
THAT LOOKS FUN, MAY I JOIN YOU?
POP
POP

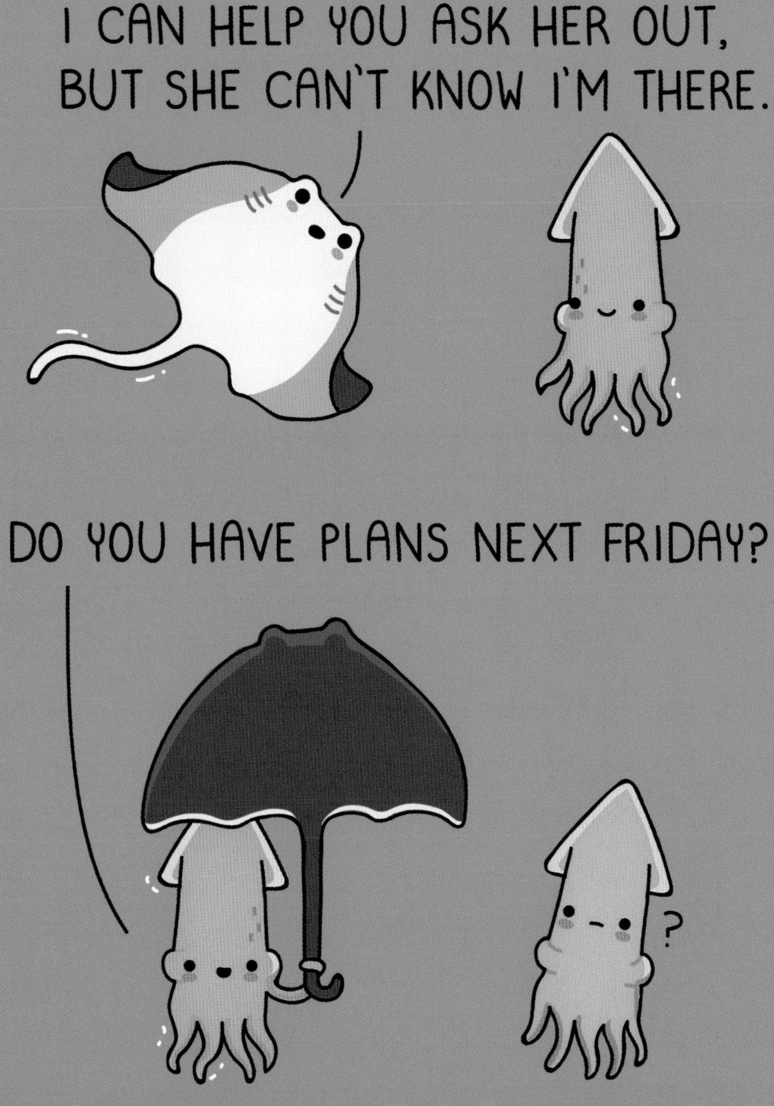
I CAN HELP YOU ASK HER OUT,
BUT SHE CAN'T KNOW I'M THERE.
DO YOU HAVE PLANS NEXT FRIDAY?
?

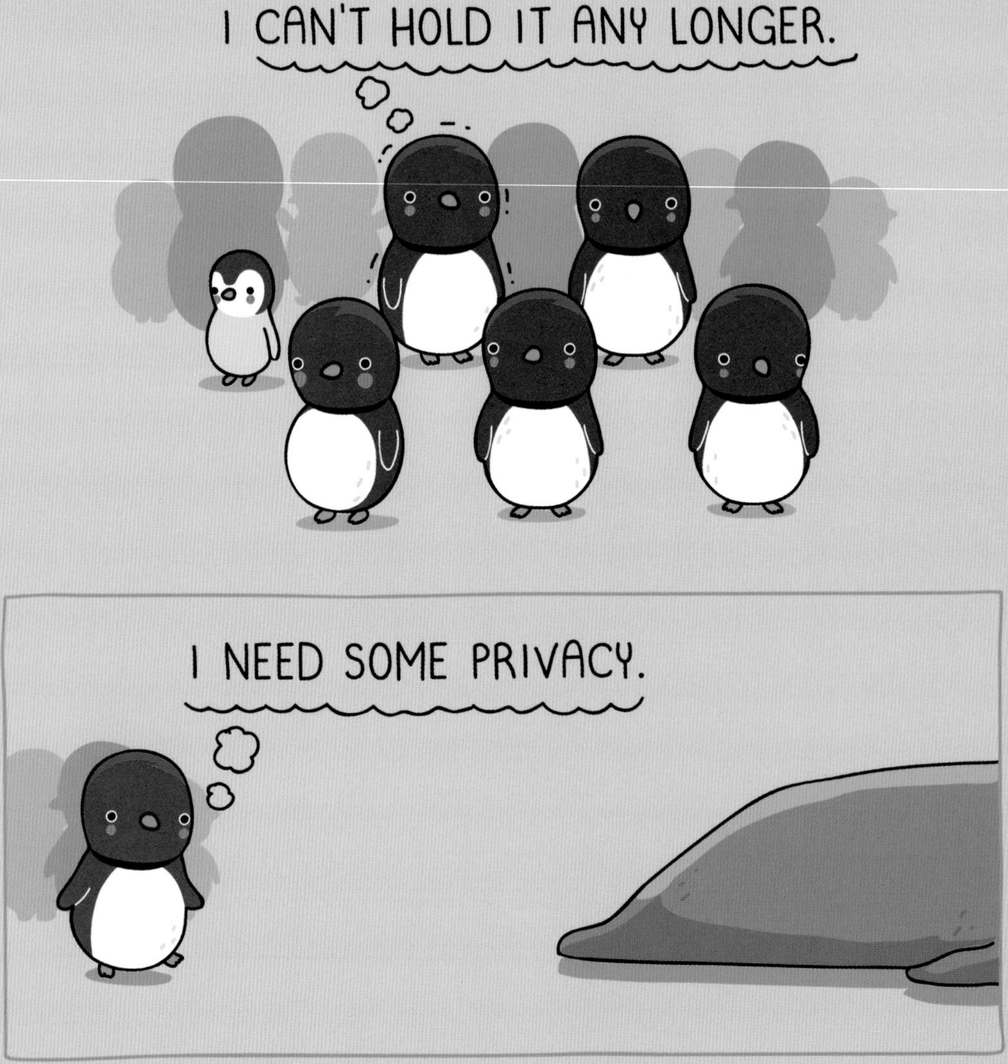
I CAN'T HOLD IT ANY LONGER.
I NEED SOME PRIVACY.

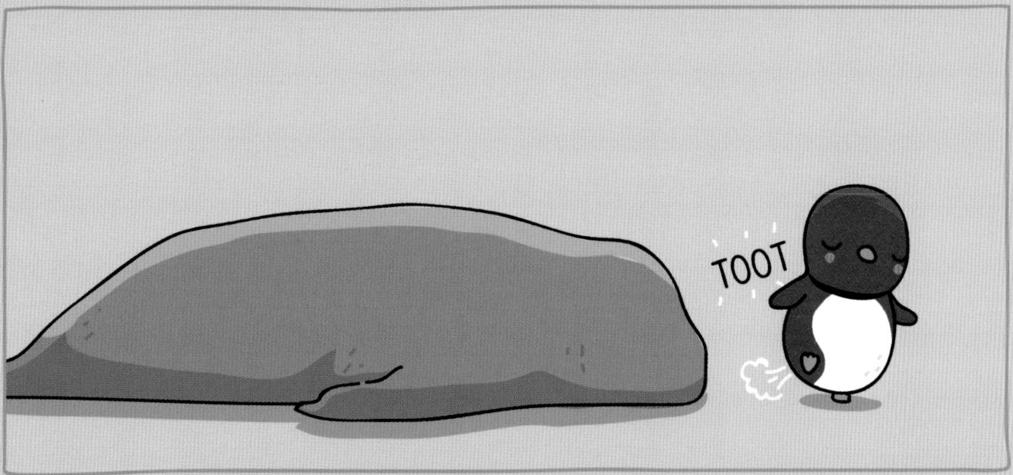
TOOT

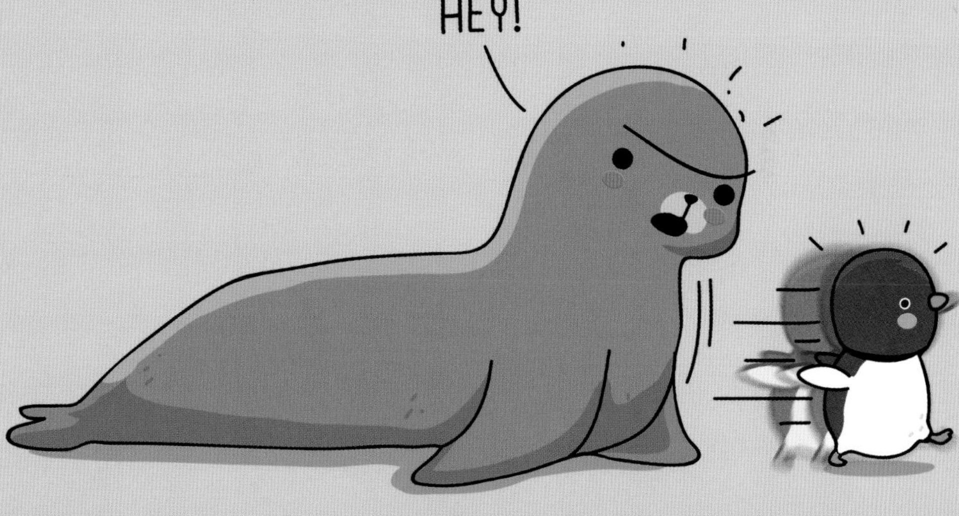
HEY!

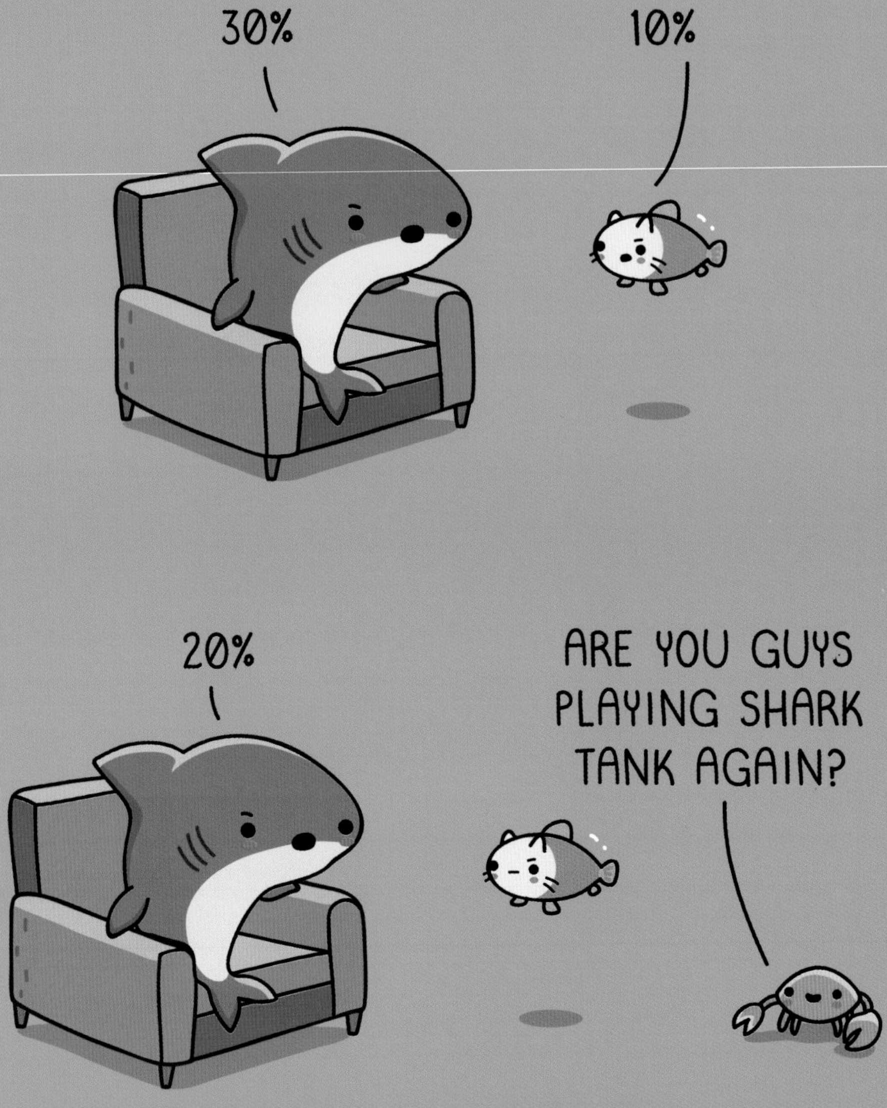
30%
10%
20%
ARE YOU GUYS PLAYING SHARK TANK AGAIN?

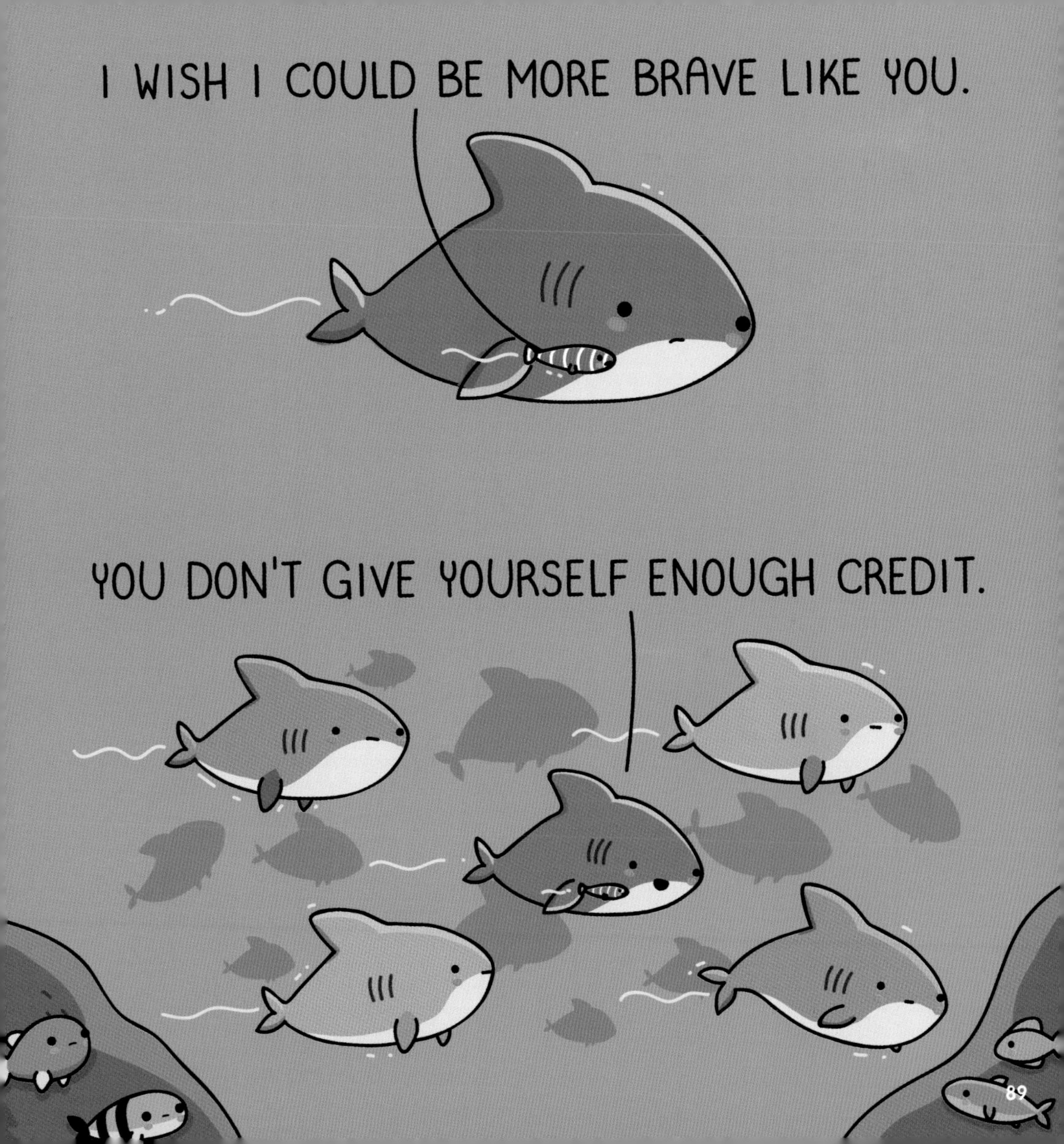
I WISH I COULD BE MORE BRAVE LIKE YOU.
YOU DON'T GIVE YOURSELF ENOUGH CREDIT.

COOKING AN EGG IS EASY. JUST FRY.

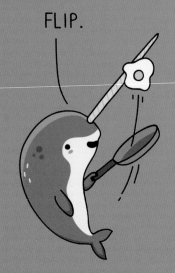

FLIP.

USE A SPATULA NEXT TIME.

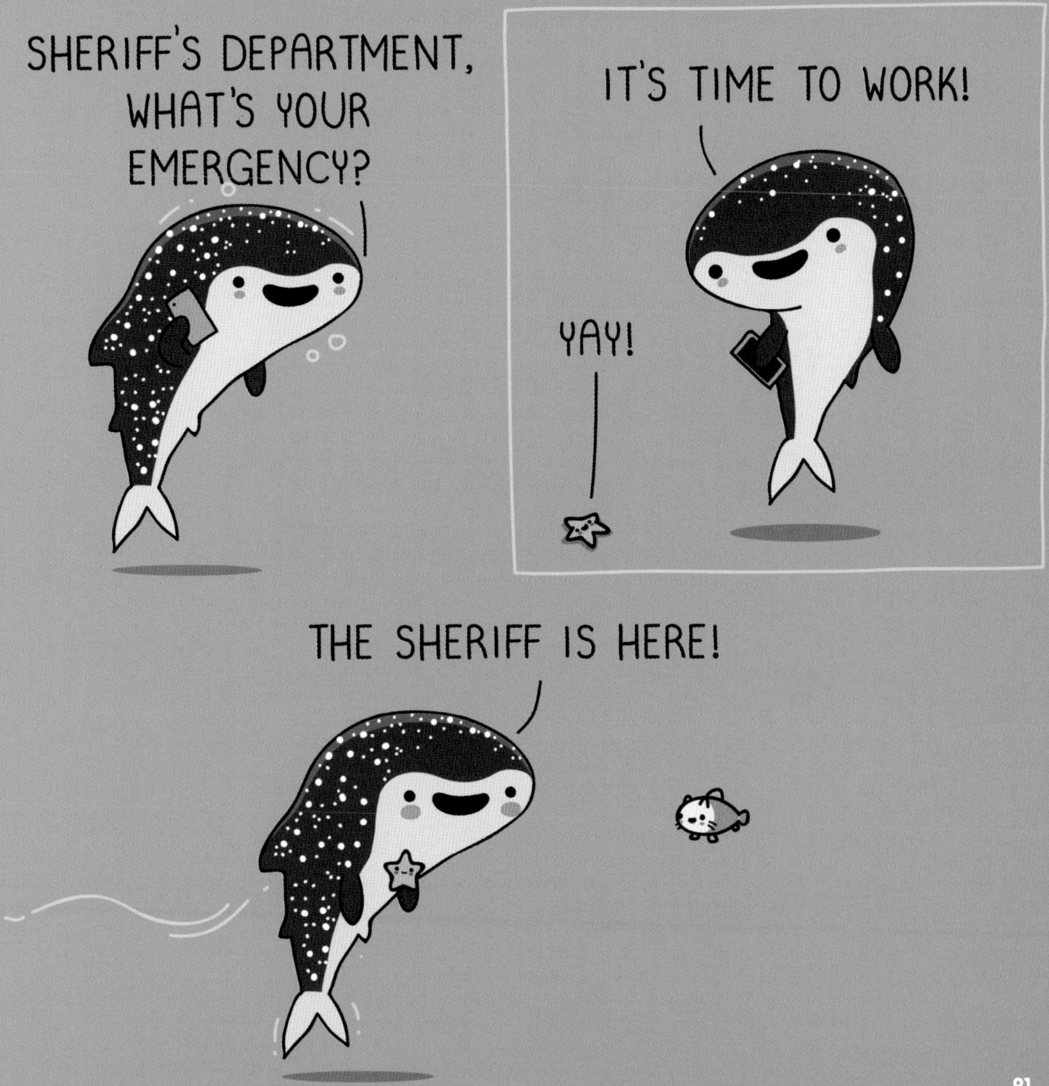
SHERIFF'S DEPARTMENT, WHAT'S YOUR EMERGENCY?
IT'S TIME TO WORK!
YAY!
THE SHERIFF IS HERE!

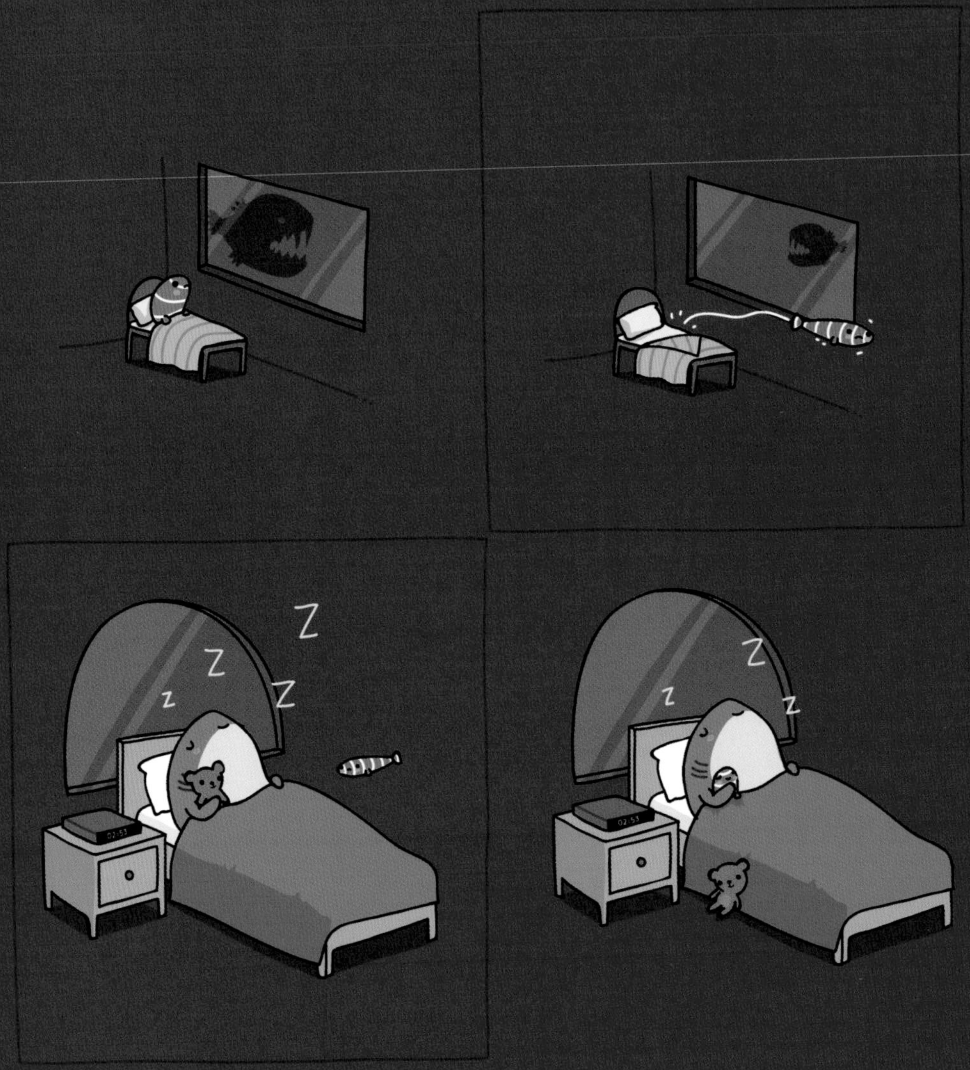
z
Z
Z
Z
z
Z
z

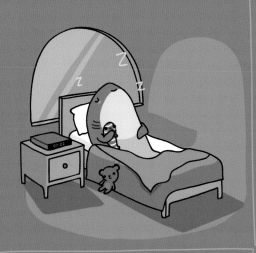

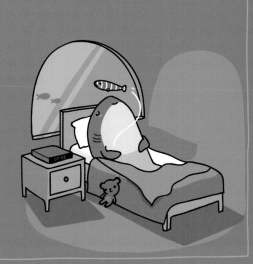

YOU DO SO MUCH FOR ME.

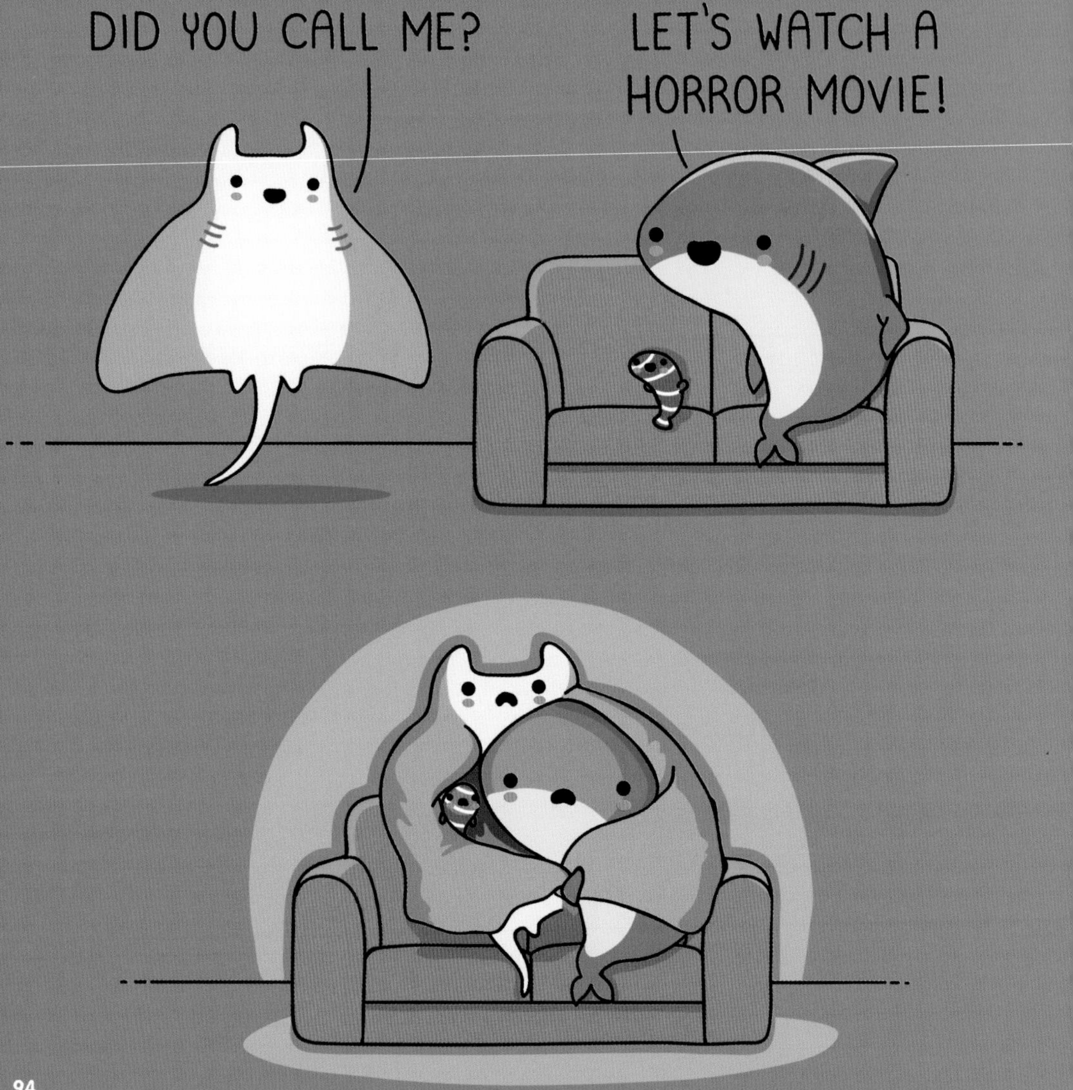
DID YOU CALL ME?
LET'S WATCH A HORROR MOVIE!

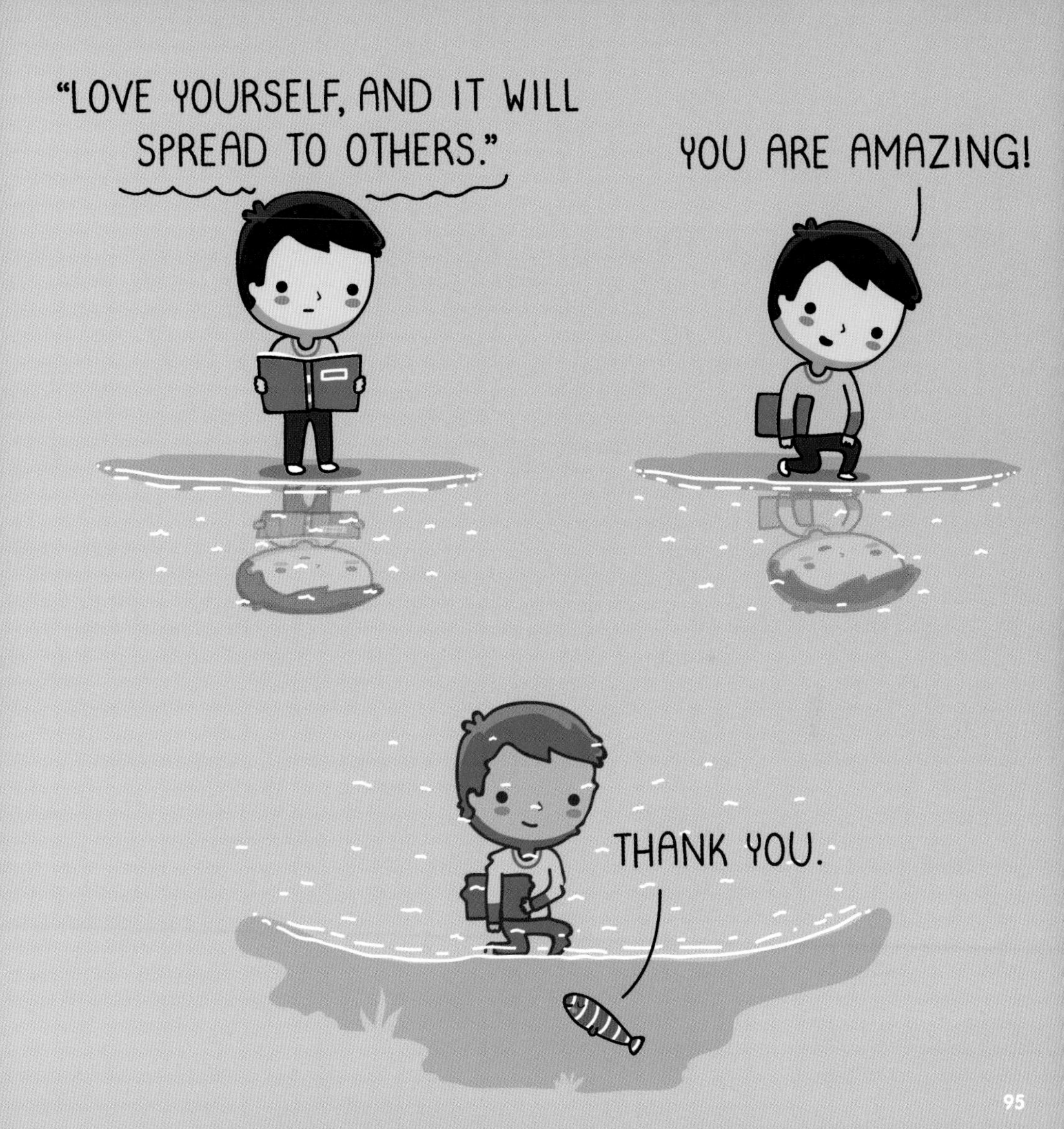
"LOVE YOURSELF, AND IT WILL SPREAD TO OTHERS."
YOU ARE AMAZING!
THANK YOU.

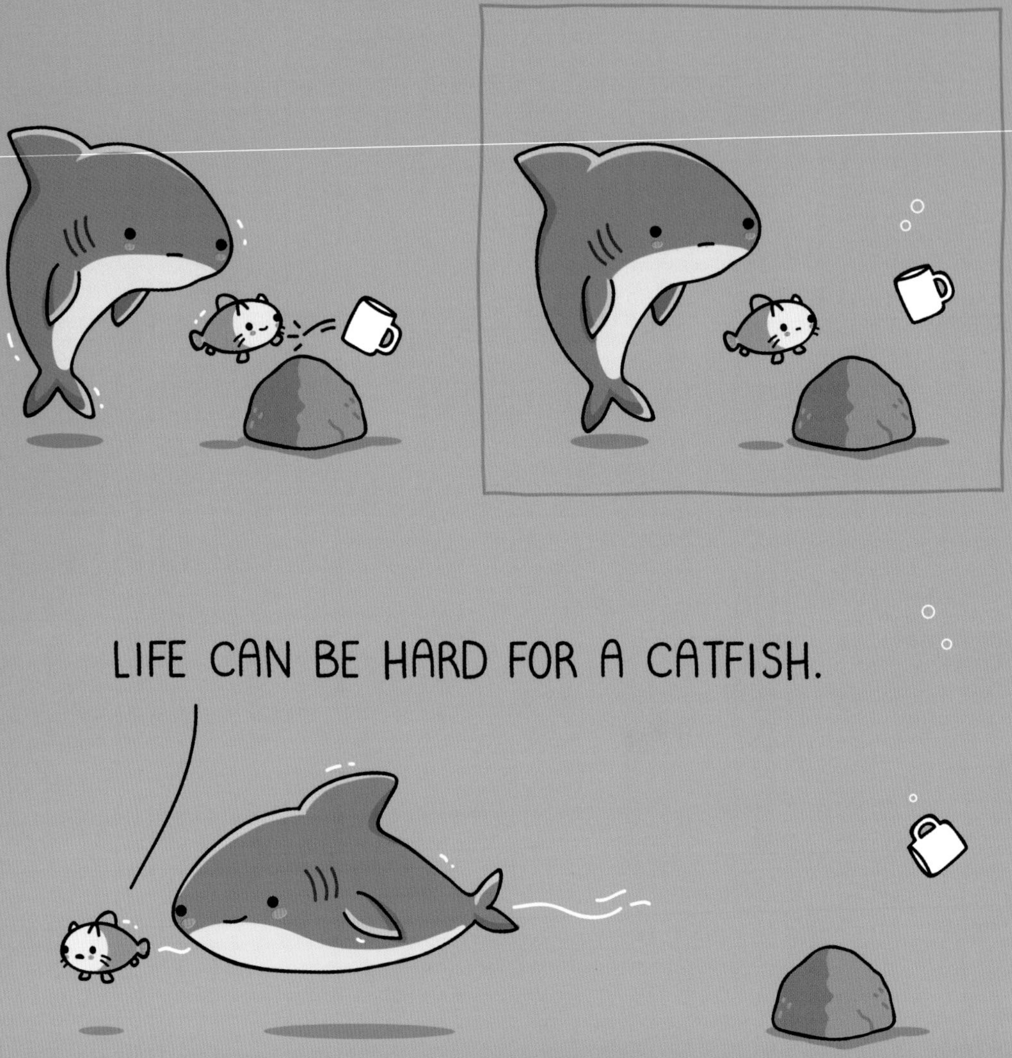
LIFE CAN BE HARD FOR A CATFISH.

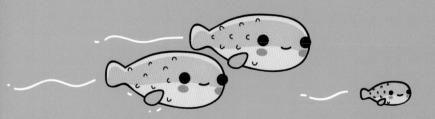

THEY GROW UP SO FAST.

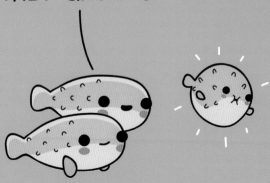

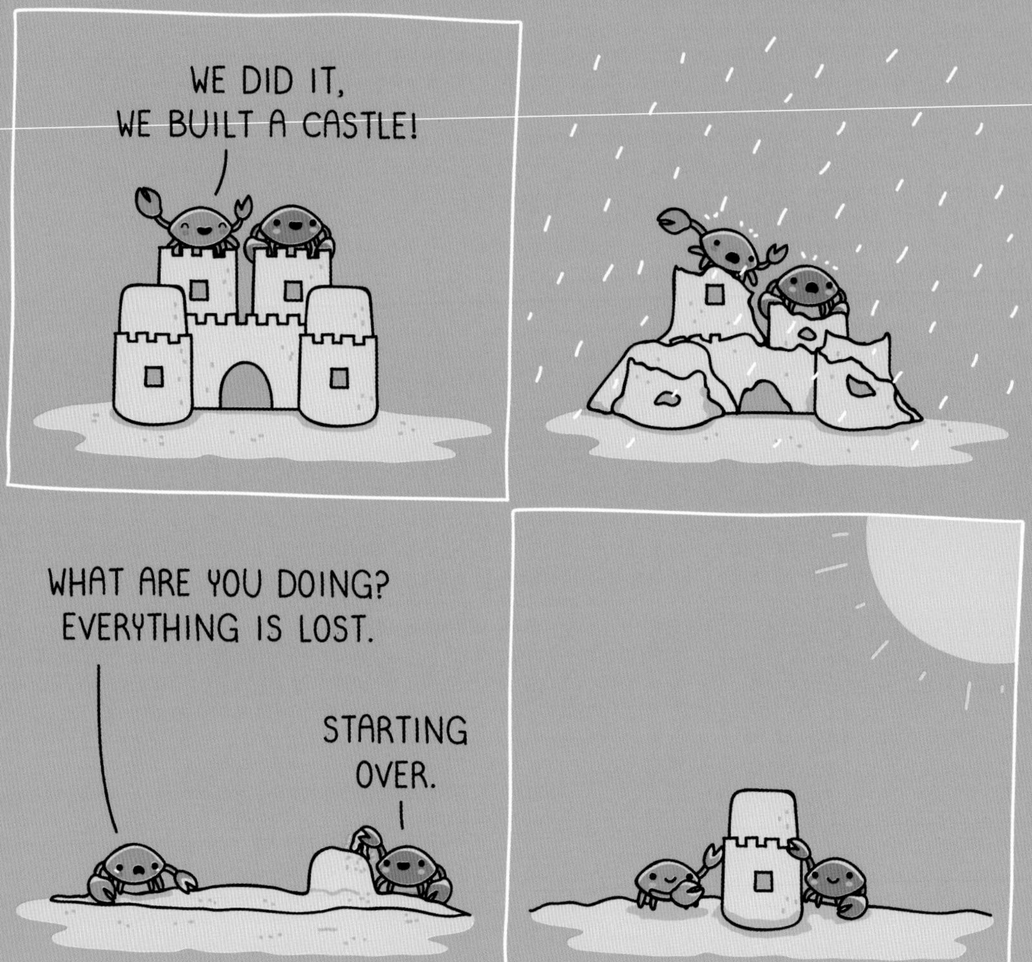
WE DID IT,
WE BUILT A CASTLE!
WHAT ARE YOU DOING?
EVERYTHING IS LOST.
STARTING
OVER.

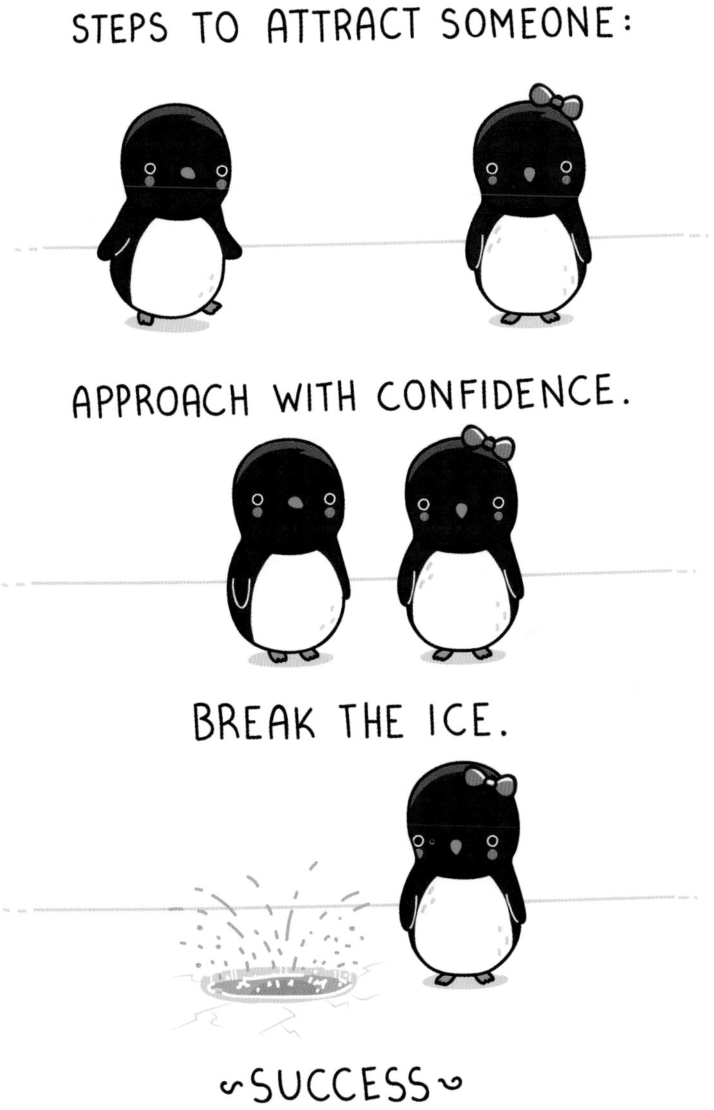
STEPS TO ATTRACT SOMEONE:
APPROACH WITH CONFIDENCE.
BREAK THE ICE.
~SUCCESS~

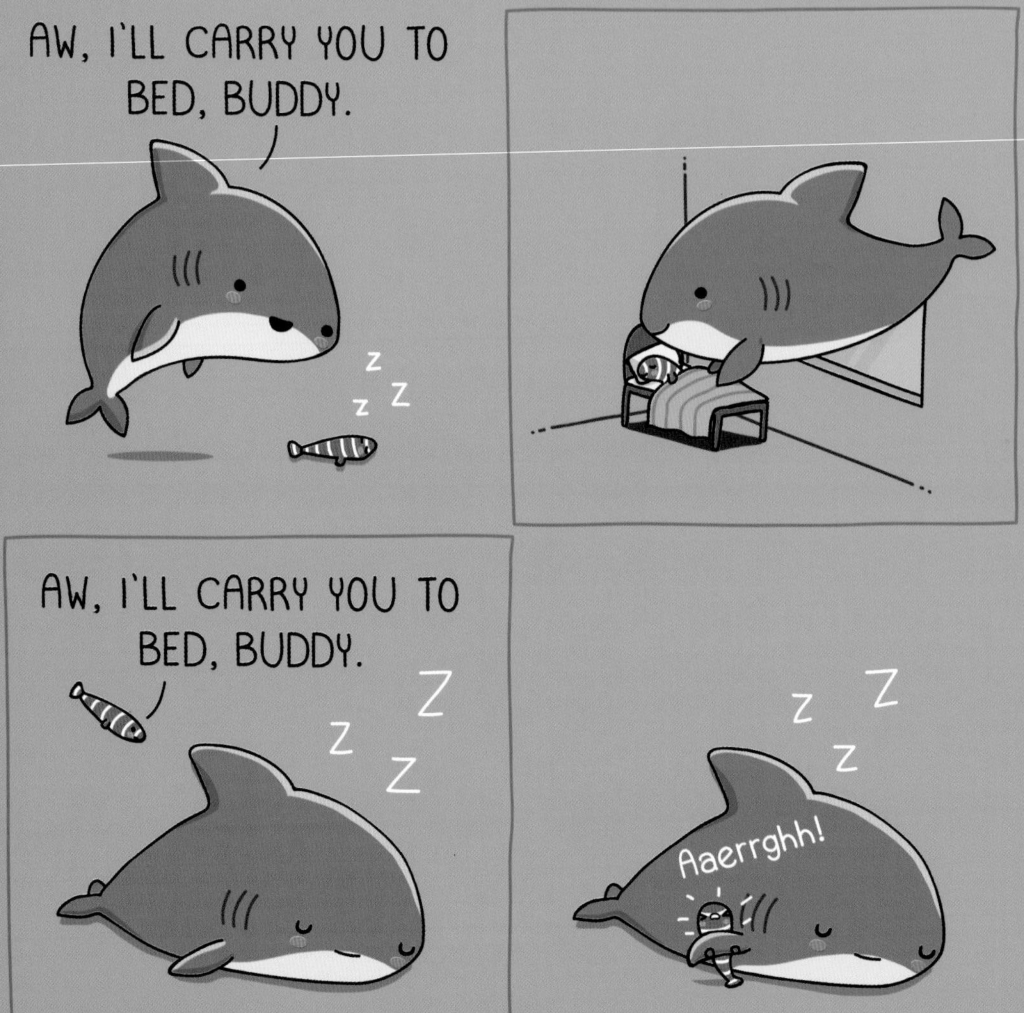

AW, I'LL CARRY YOU TO BED, BUDDY.
Z Z Z
AW, I'LL CARRY YOU TO BED, BUDDY.
Z Z Z
Z Z Z
Aaerrghh!

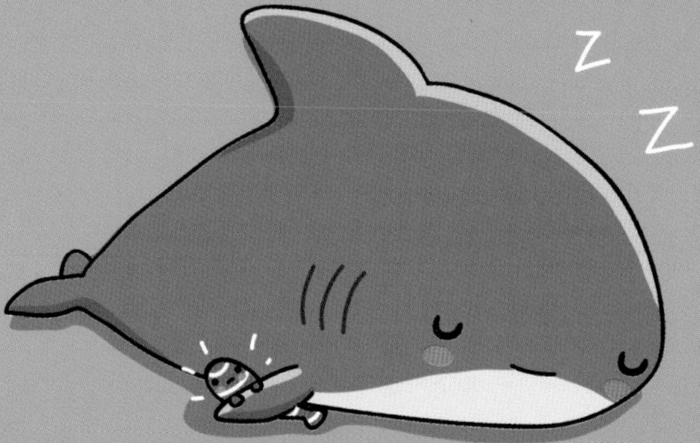
Z
Z

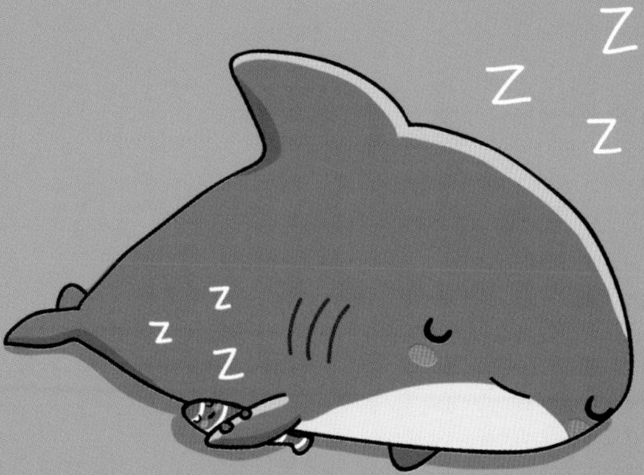
Z
Z
Z
Z
Z
Z

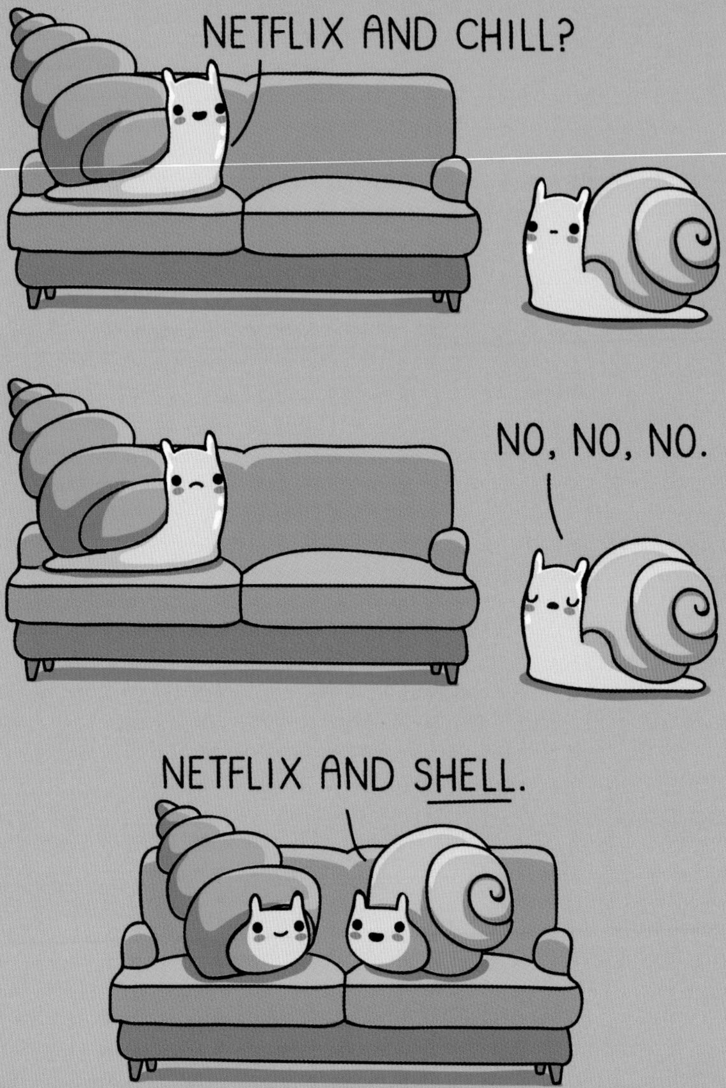
NETFLIX AND CHILL?
NO, NO, NO.
NETFLIX AND SHELL.

HUH!? WHO'S THERE?

DUDE, IT'S ALMOST MIDNIGHT.

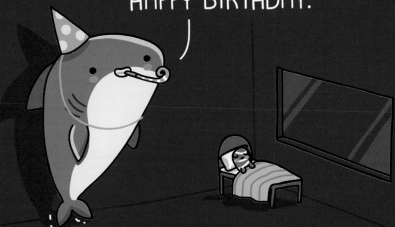

I WANNA BE THE FIRST TO SAY HAPPY BIRTHDAY.

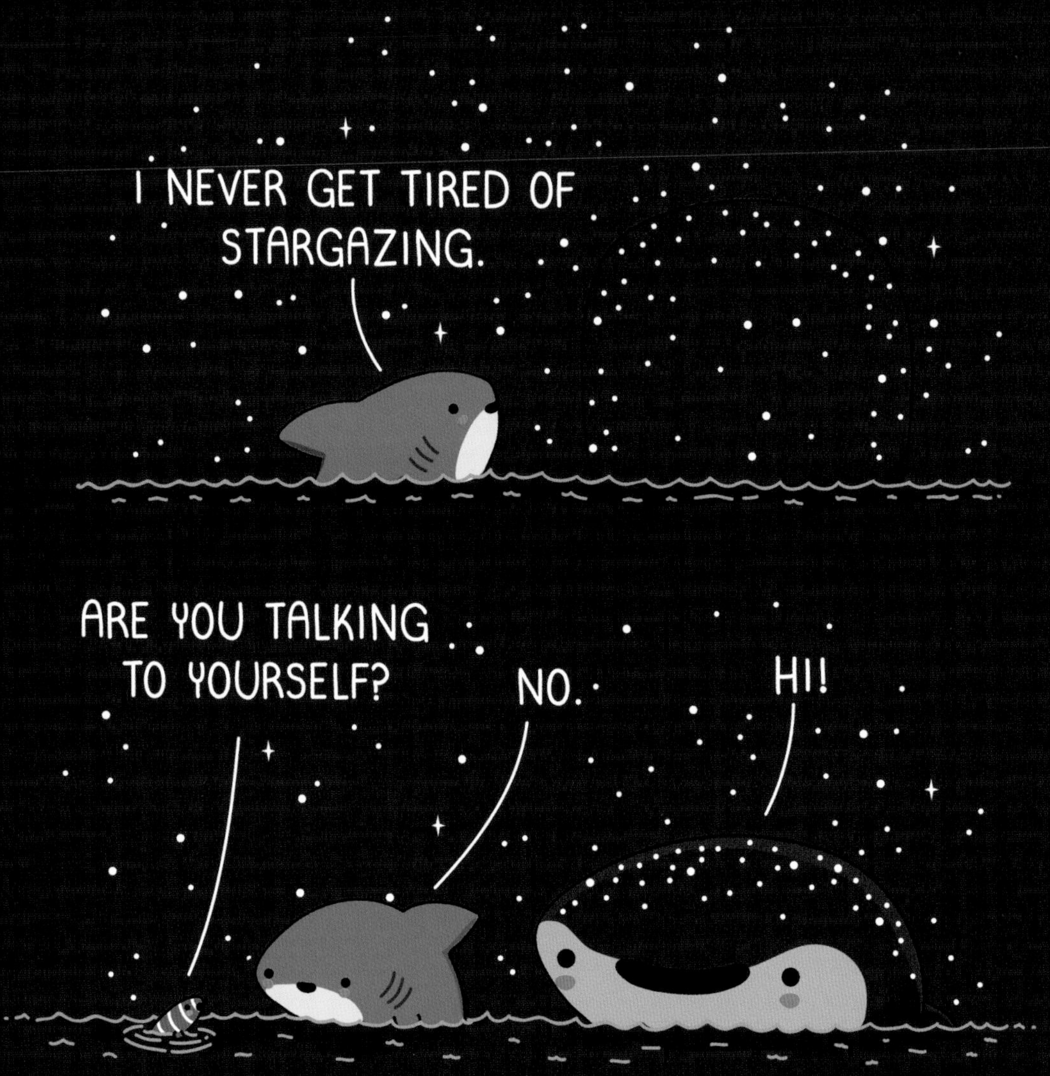
I NEVER GET TIRED OF STARGAZING.
ARE YOU TALKING TO YOURSELF?
NO.
HI!

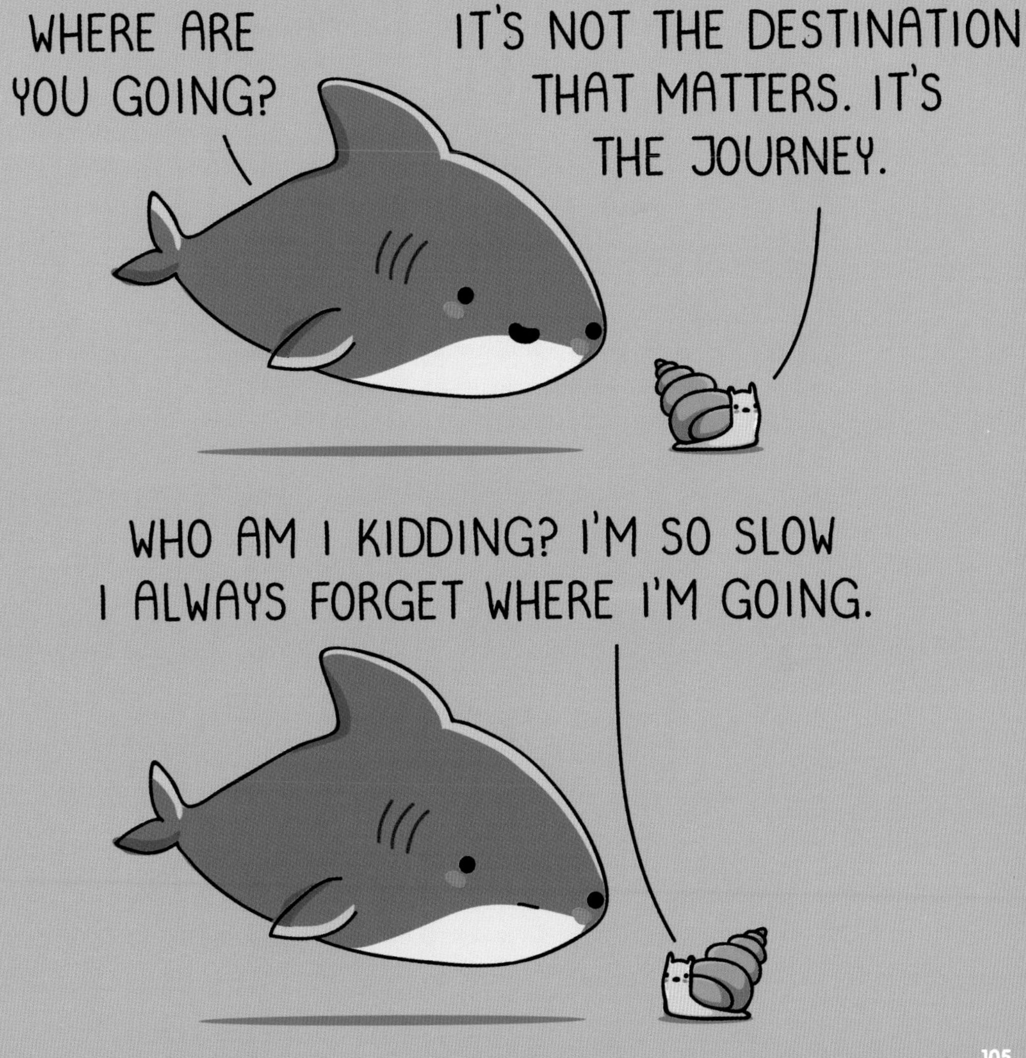
WHERE ARE YOU GOING?
IT'S NOT THE DESTINATION THAT MATTERS. IT'S THE JOURNEY.
WHO AM I KIDDING? I'M SO SLOW I ALWAYS FORGET WHERE I'M GOING.

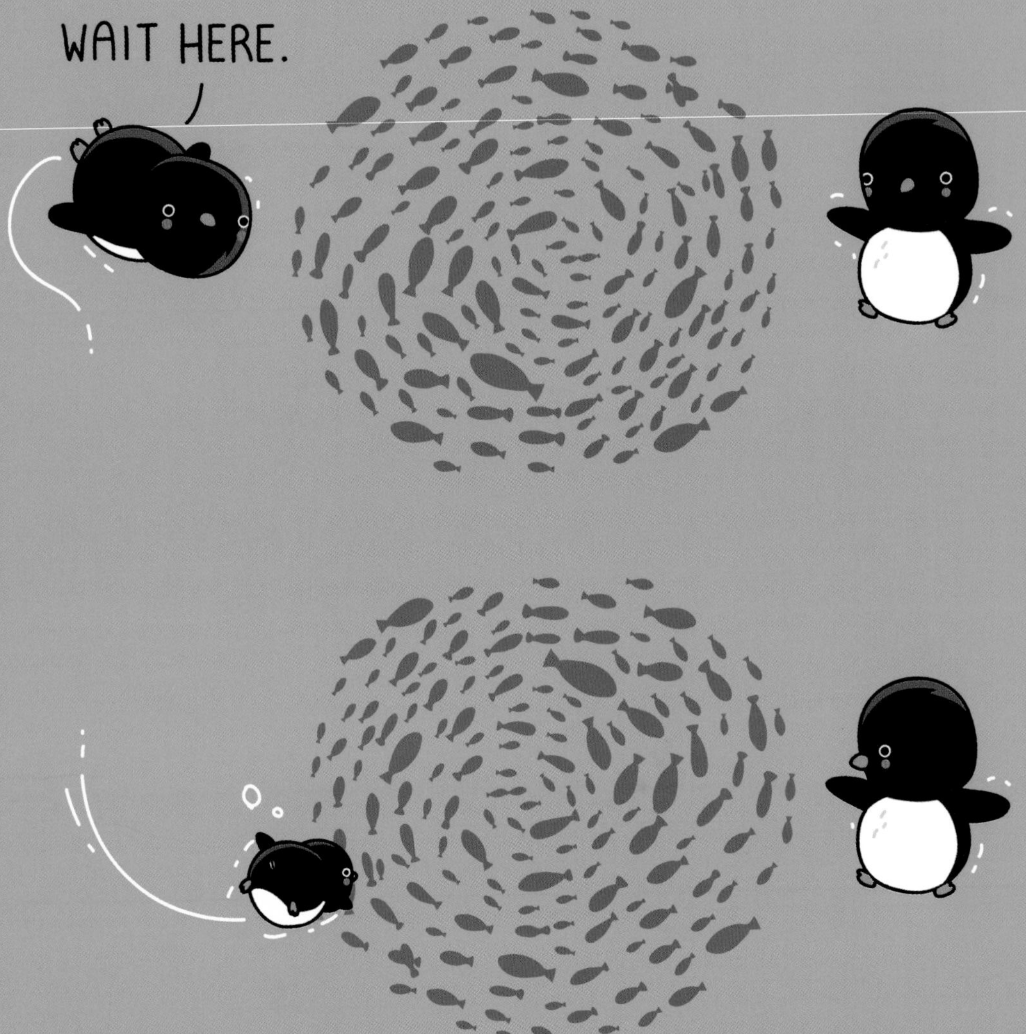
WAIT HERE.

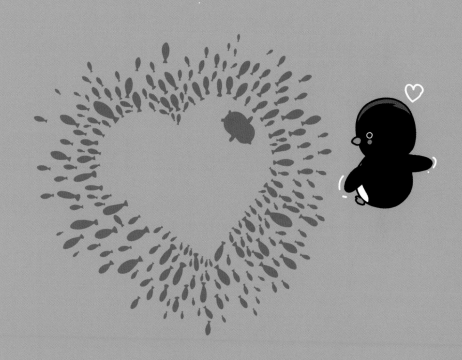

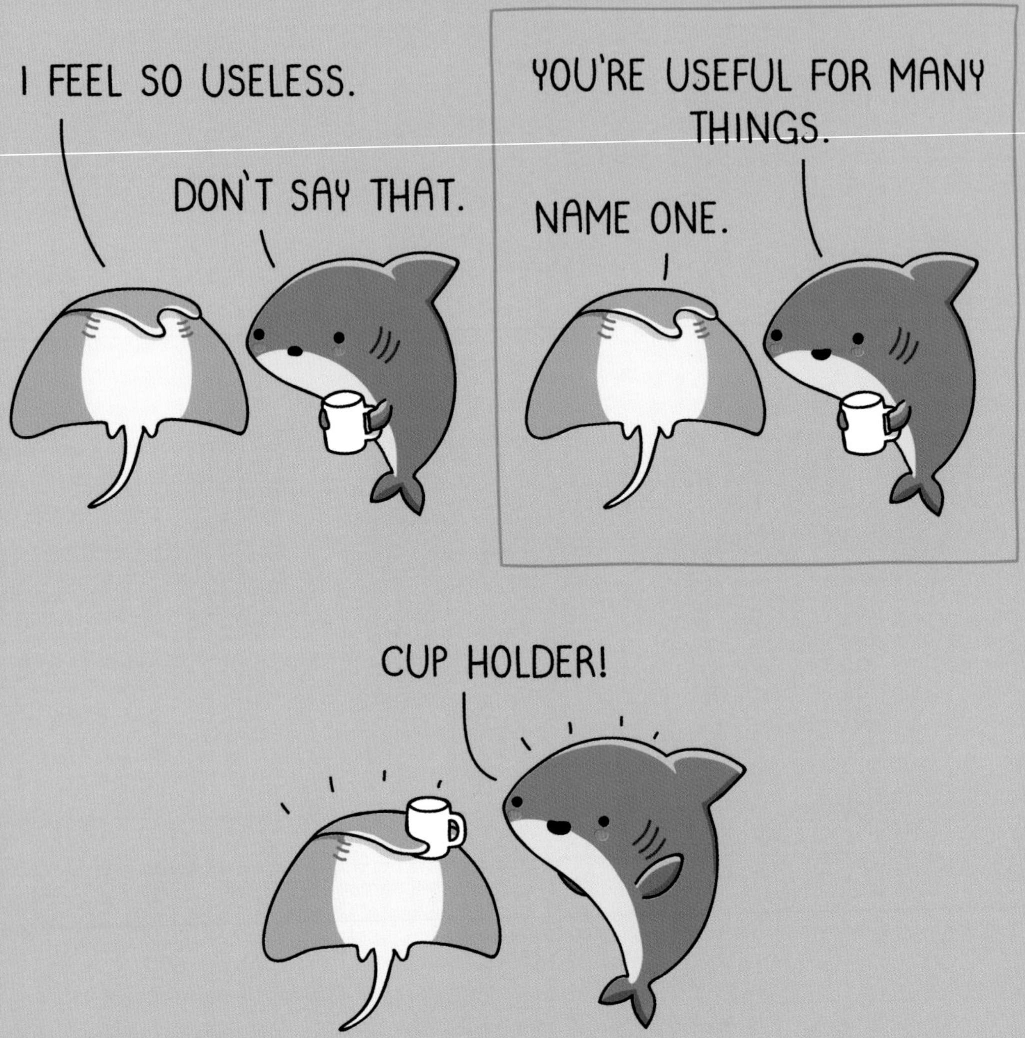
I FEEL SO USELESS.
DON'T SAY THAT.
YOU'RE USEFUL FOR MANY THINGS.
NAME ONE.
CUP HOLDER!

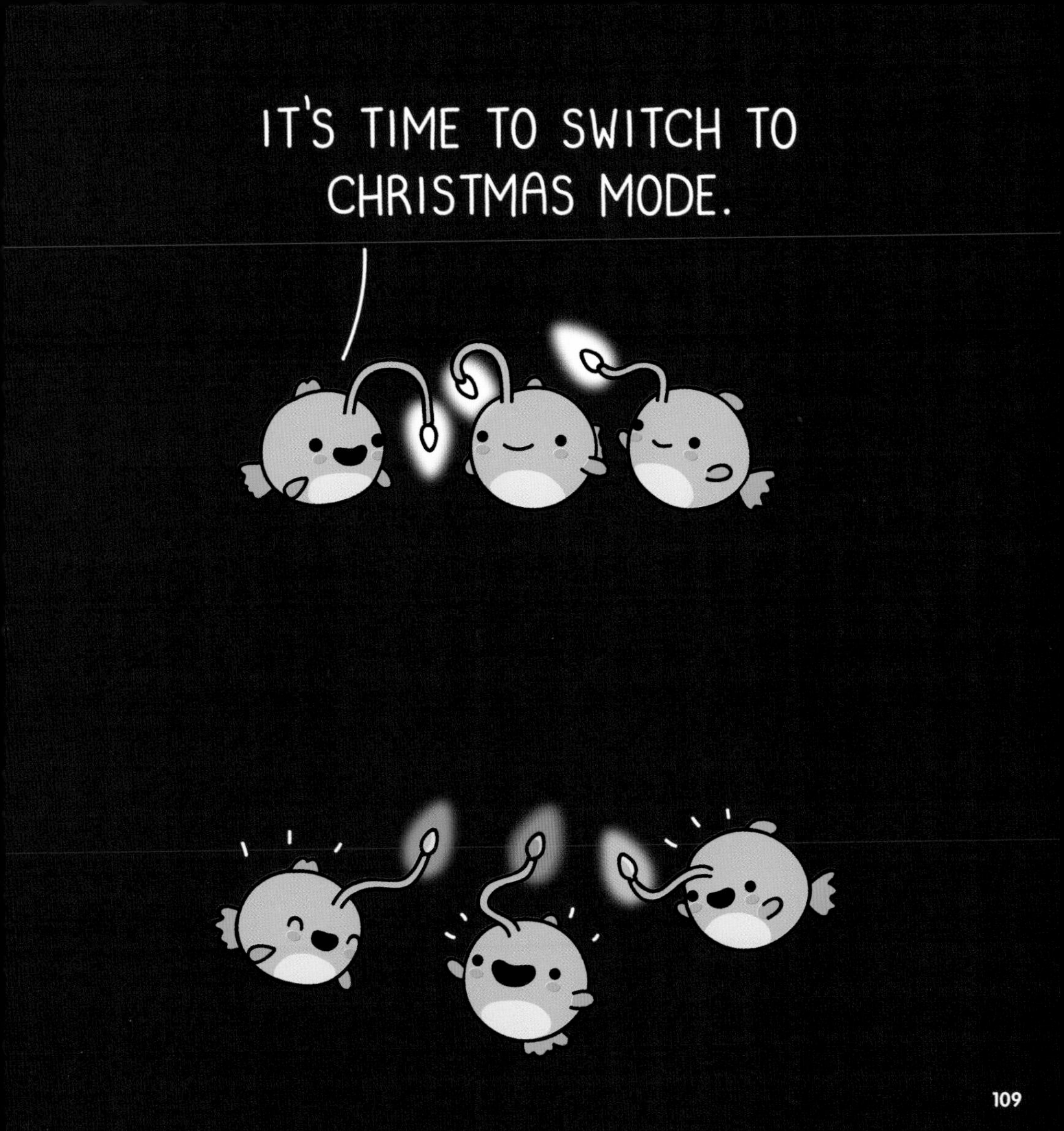
IT'S TIME TO SWITCH TO CHRISTMAS MODE.

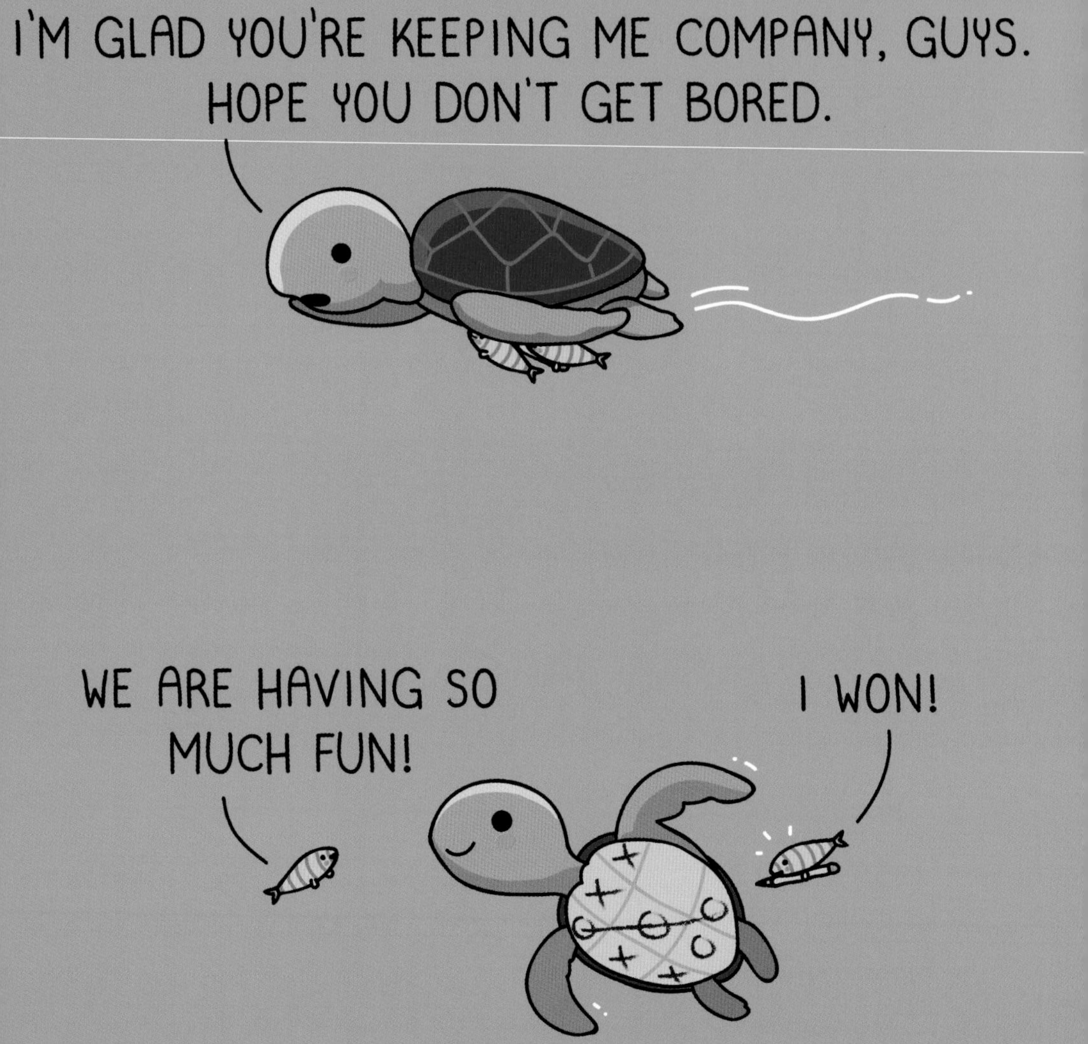
I'M GLAD YOU'RE KEEPING ME COMPANY, GUYS. HOPE YOU DON'T GET BORED.
WE ARE HAVING SO MUCH FUN!
I WON!

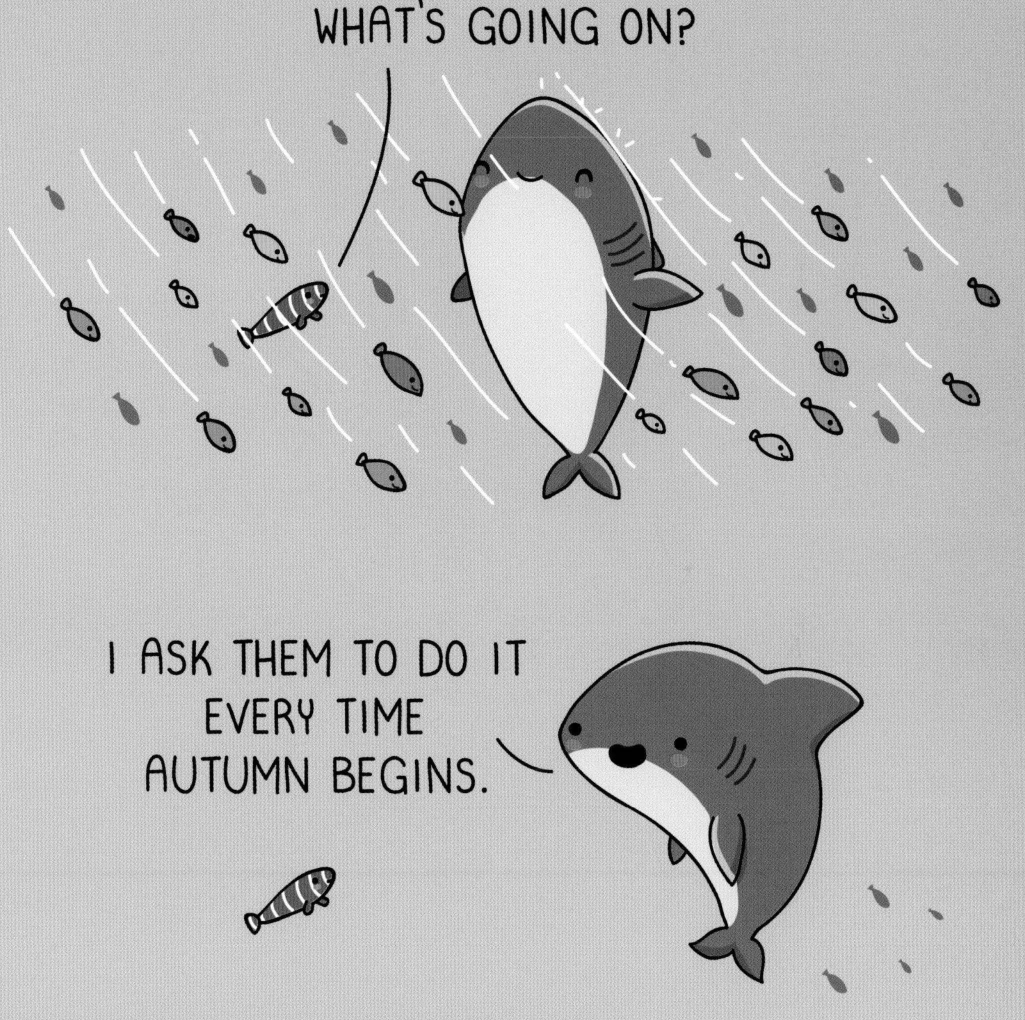
WHAT'S GOING ON?
I ASK THEM TO DO IT EVERY TIME AUTUMN BEGINS.

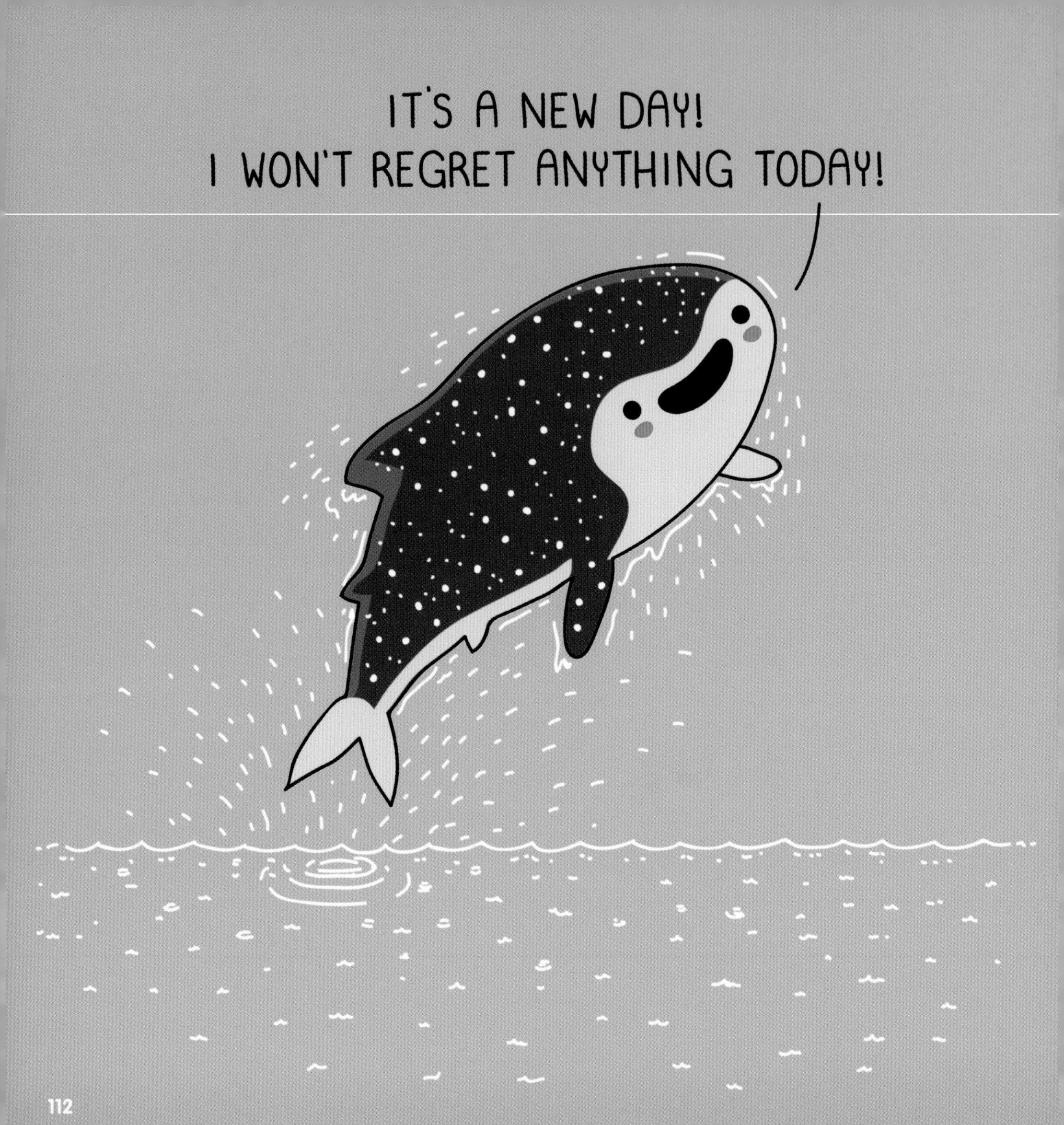
IT'S A NEW DAY!
I WON'T REGRET ANYTHING TODAY!

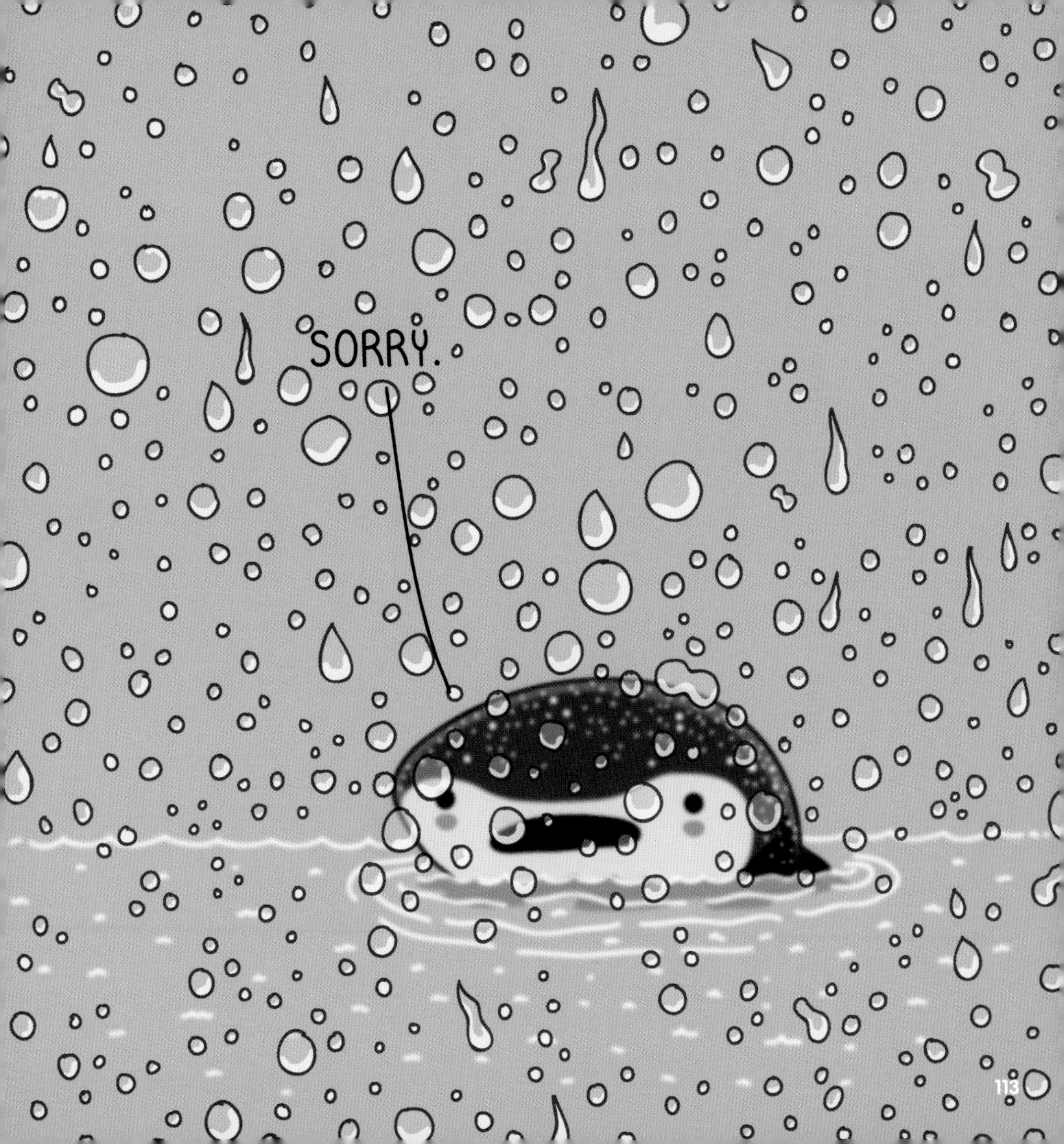
SORRY.

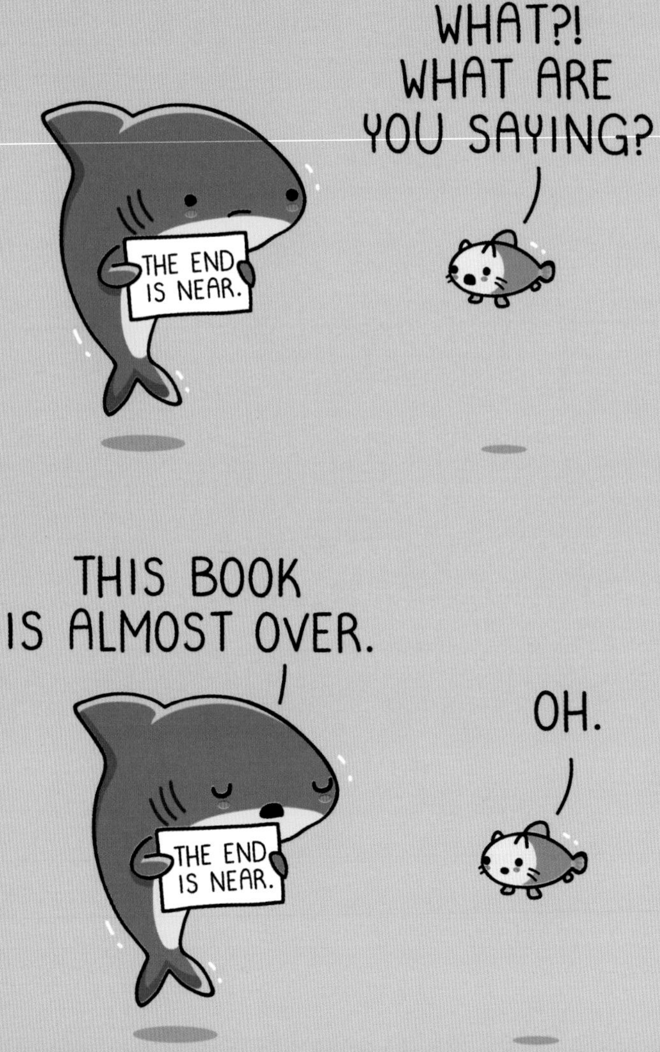
WHAT?! WHAT ARE YOU SAYING?
THE END IS NEAR.
THIS BOOK IS ALMOST OVER.
THE END IS NEAR.
OH.

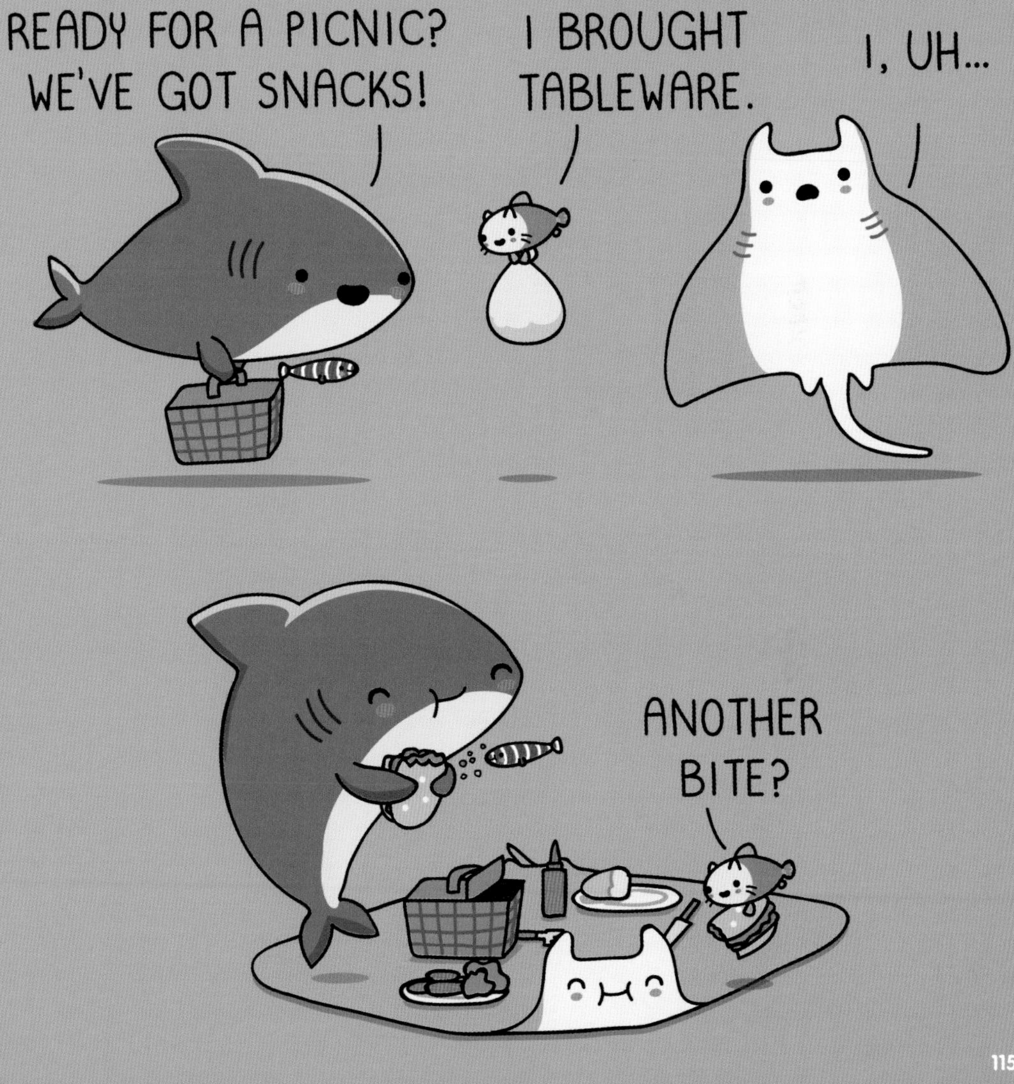
READY FOR A PICNIC? WE'VE GOT SNACKS!
I BROUGHT TABLEWARE.
I, UH...
ANOTHER BITE?

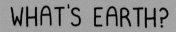

EARTH IS SUCH A
BEAUTIFUL PLACE.

WHAT'S EARTH?

IT'S WHERE WE LIVE.

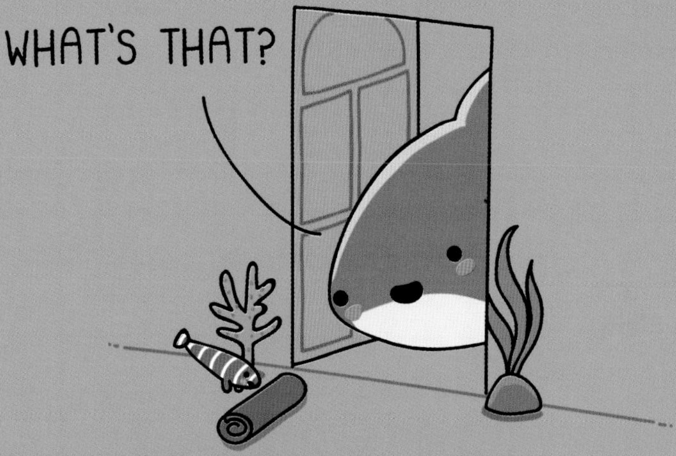
WHAT'S THAT?

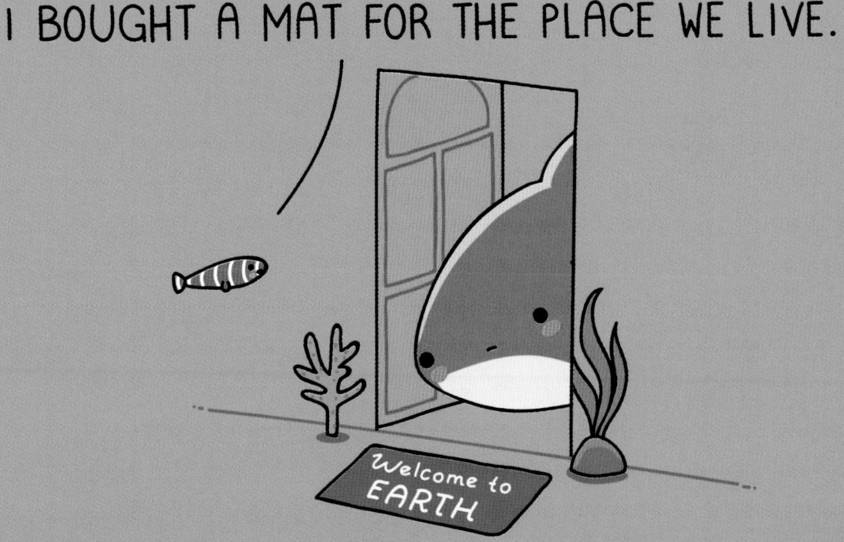
I BOUGHT A MAT FOR THE PLACE WE LIVE.
Welcome to
EARTH

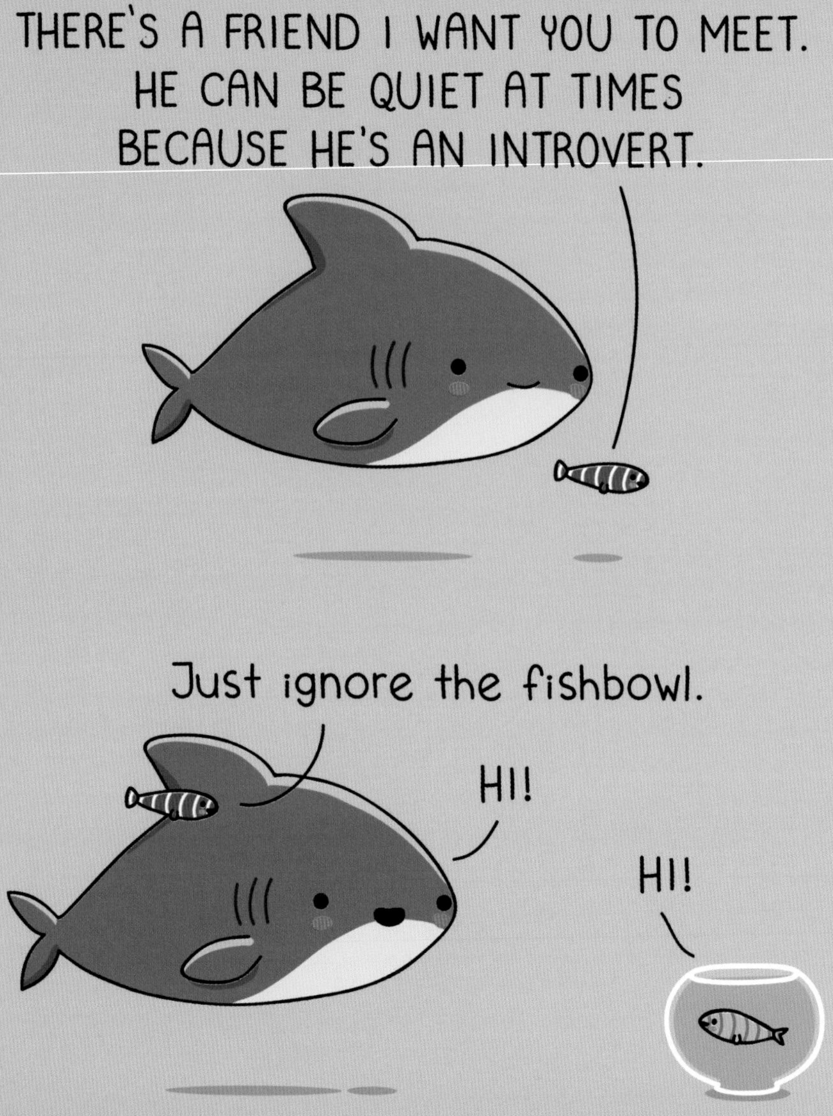
THERE'S A FRIEND I WANT YOU TO MEET. HE CAN BE QUIET AT TIMES BECAUSE HE'S AN INTROVERT.
Just ignore the fishbowl.
HI!
HI!

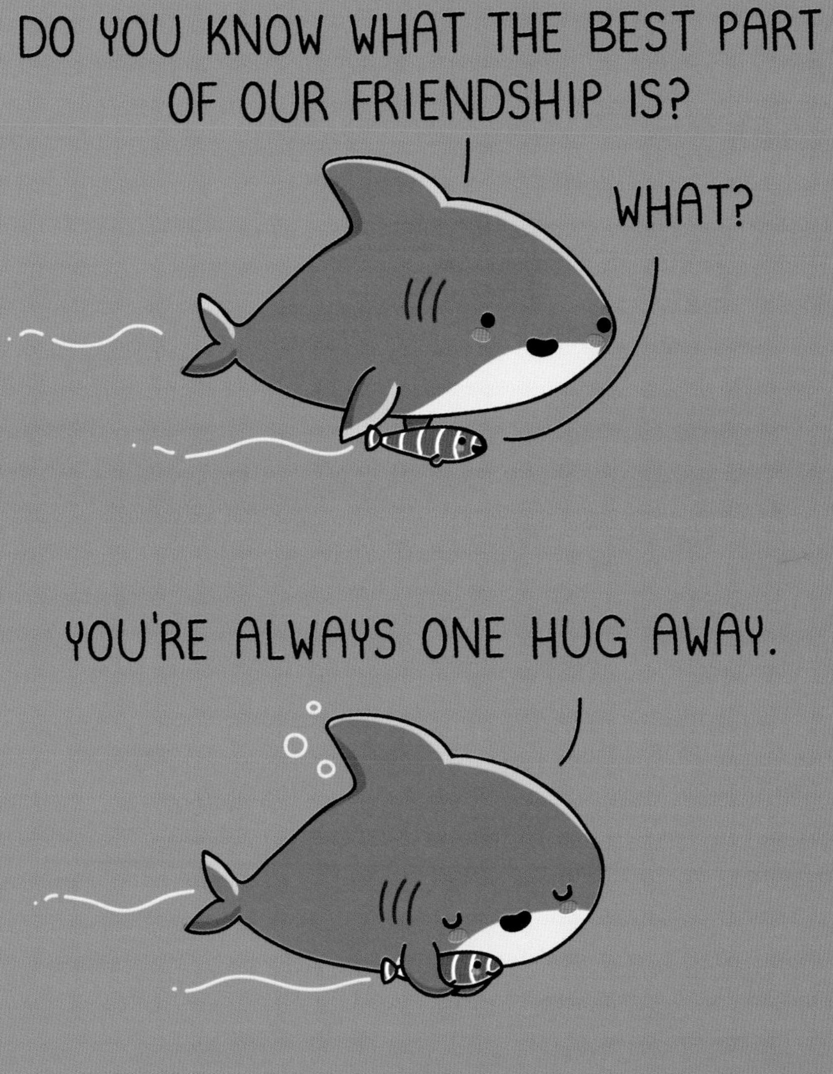
DO YOU KNOW WHAT THE BEST PART OF OUR FRIENDSHIP IS?
WHAT?
YOU'RE ALWAYS ONE HUG AWAY.

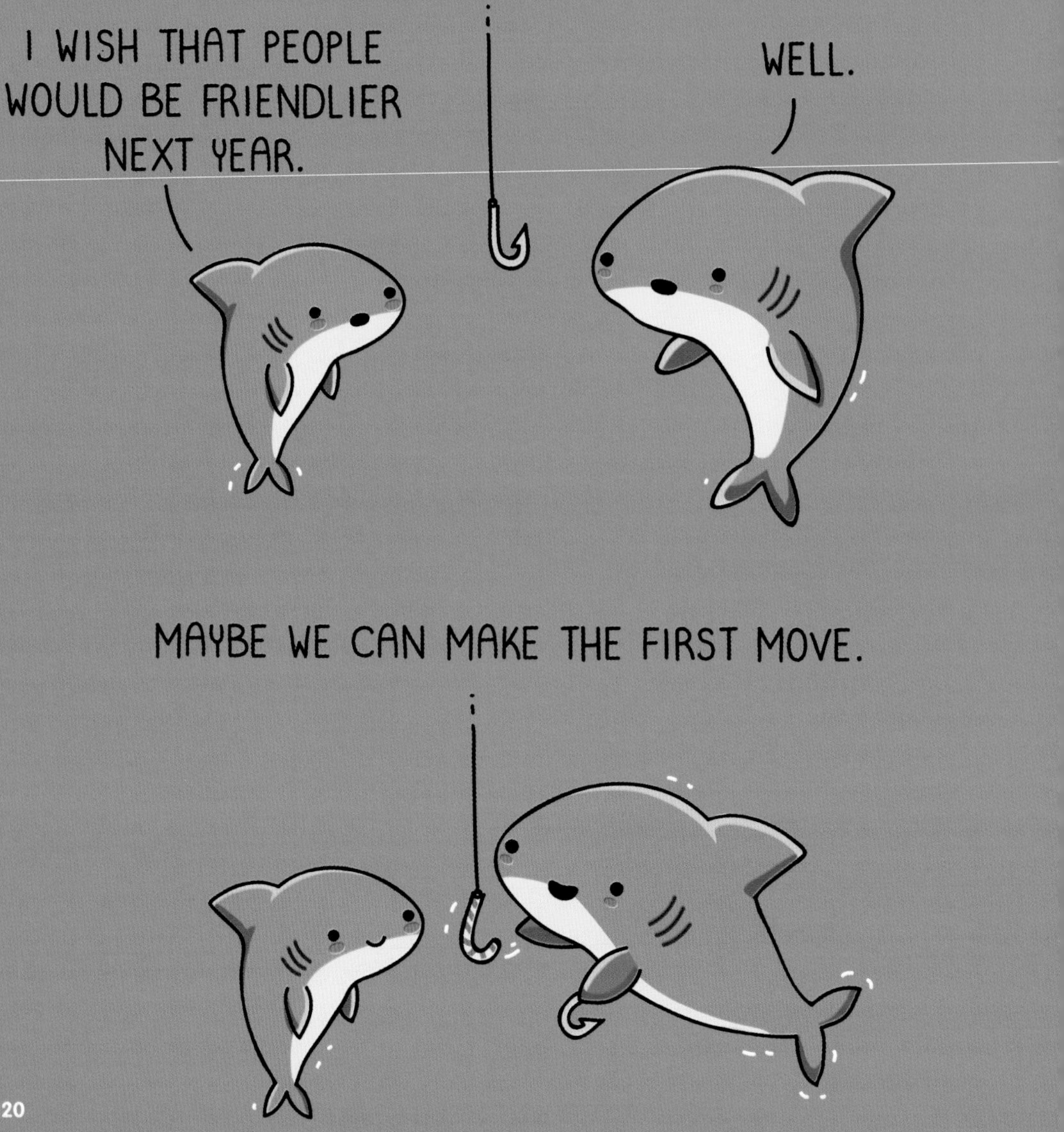
I WISH THAT PEOPLE WOULD BE FRIENDLIER NEXT YEAR.
WELL.
MAYBE WE CAN MAKE THE FIRST MOVE.

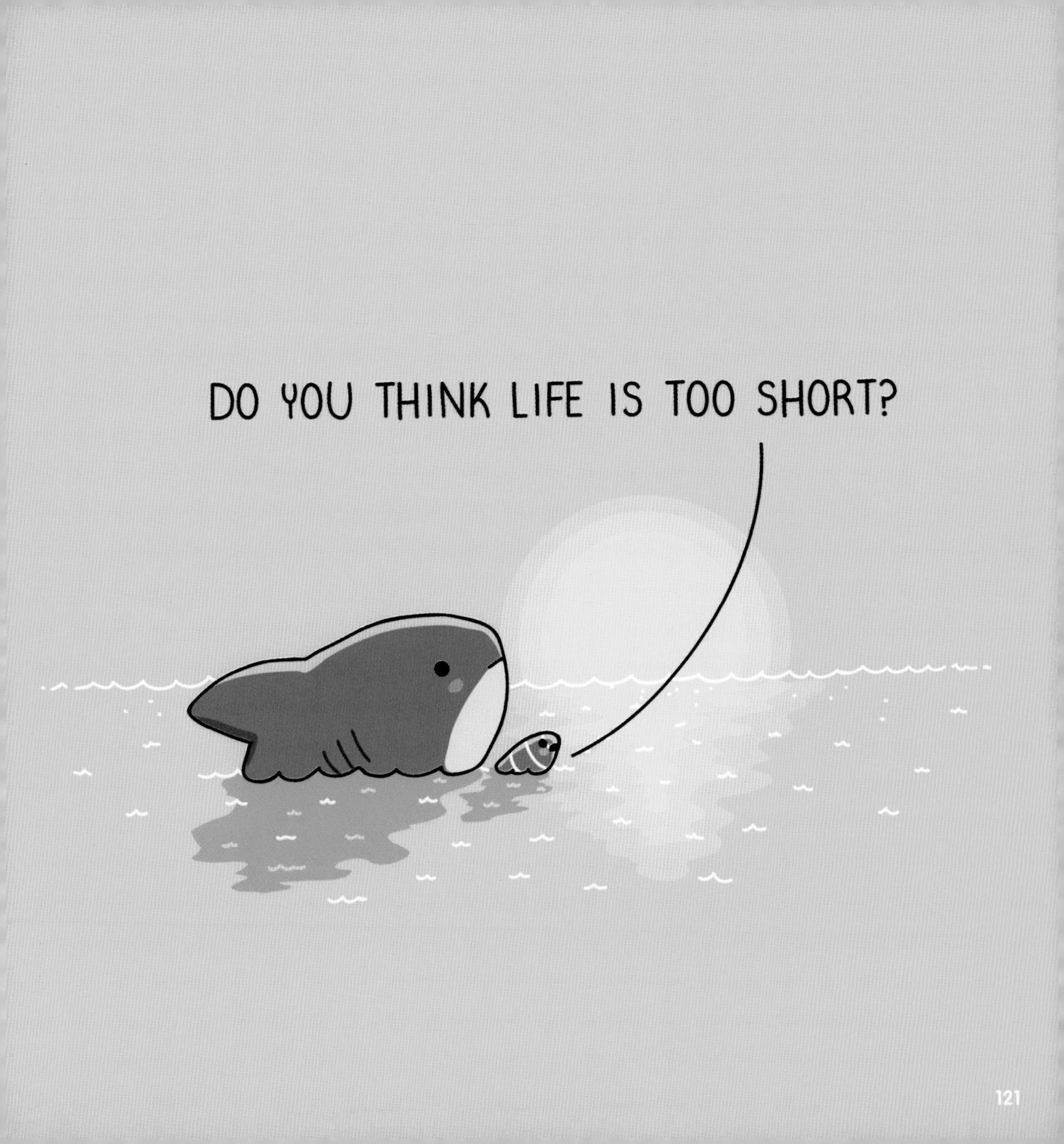
DO YOU THINK LIFE IS TOO SHORT?

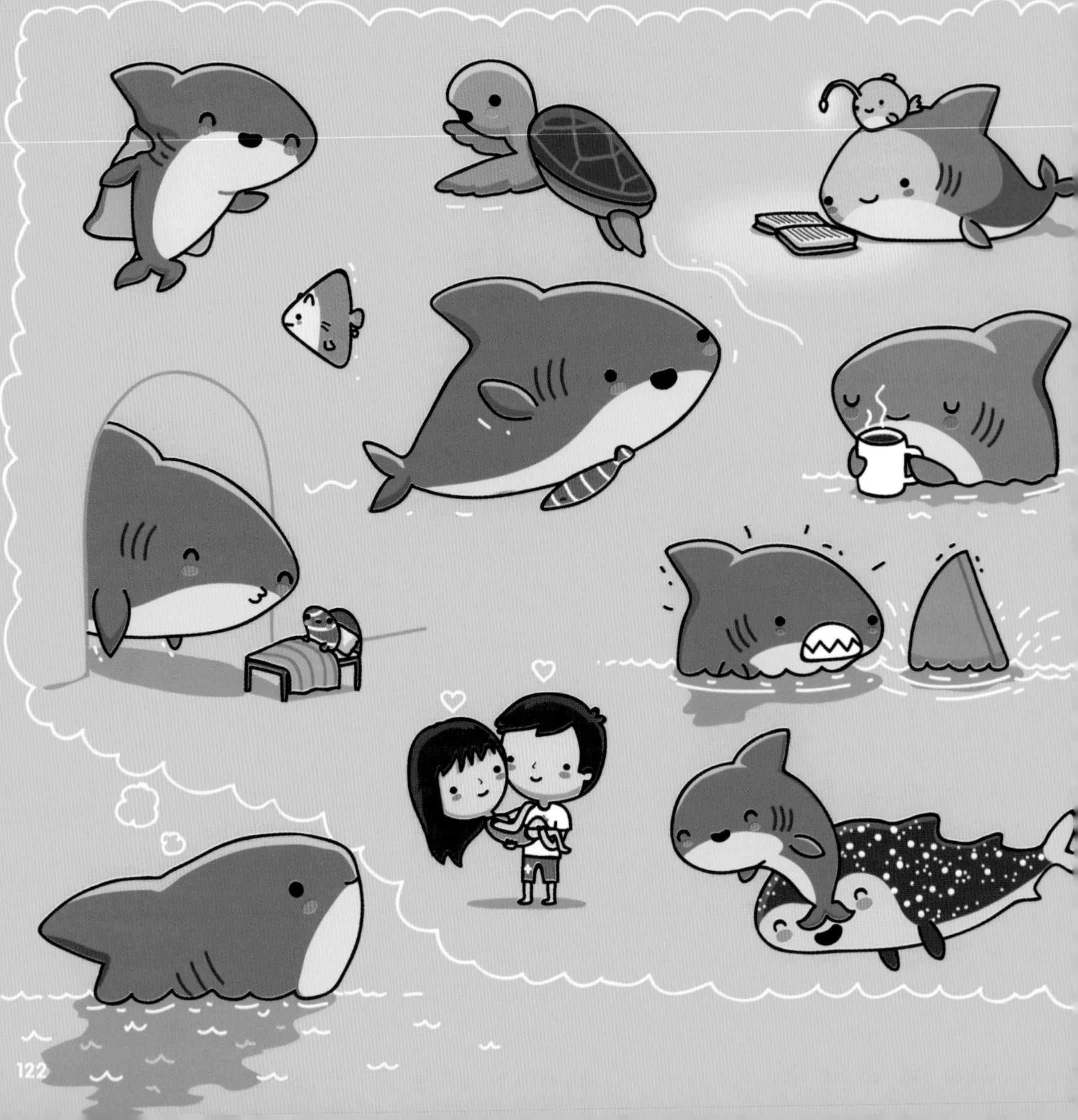

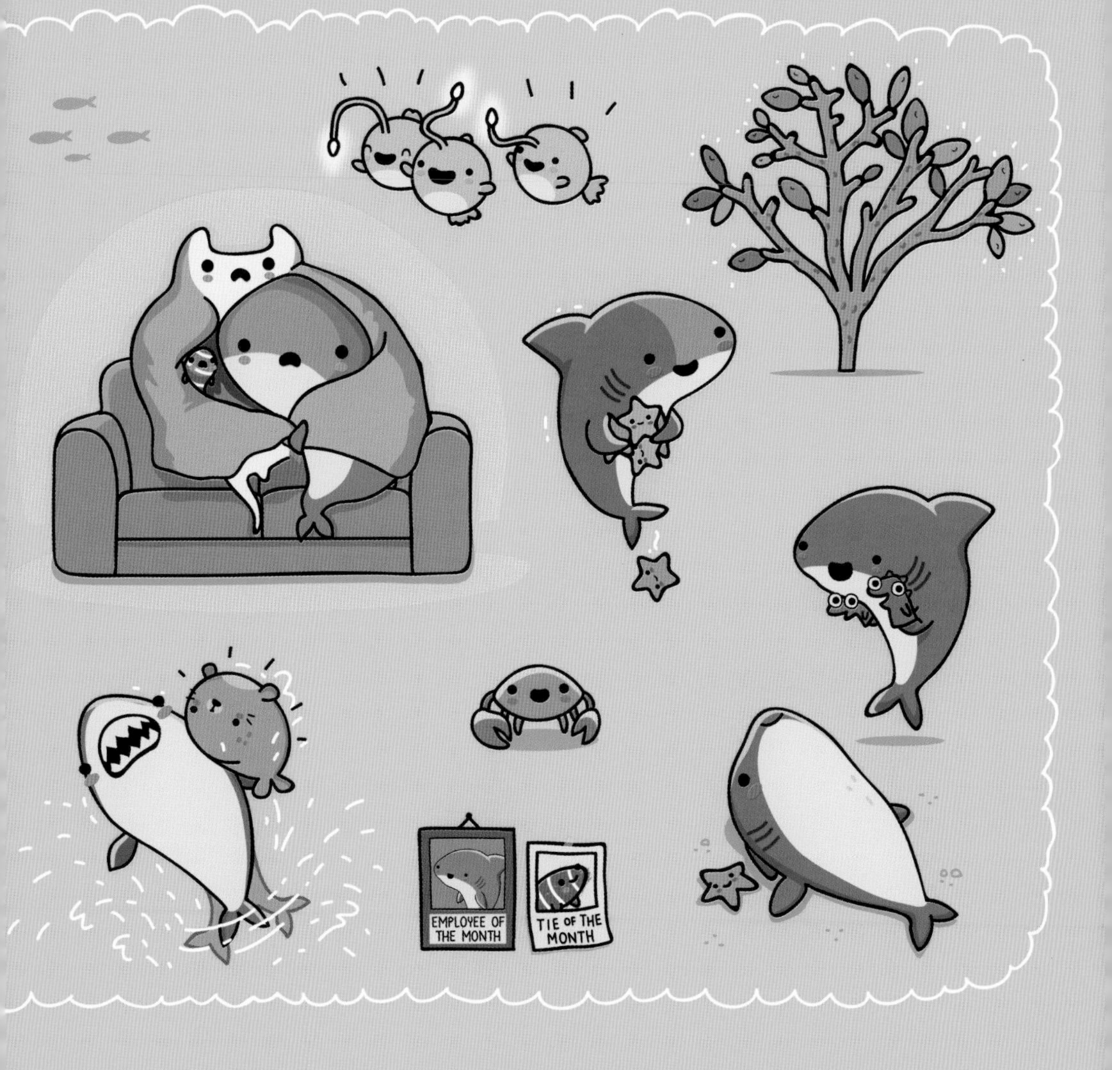
EMPLOYEE OF THE MONTH
TIE OF THE MONTH

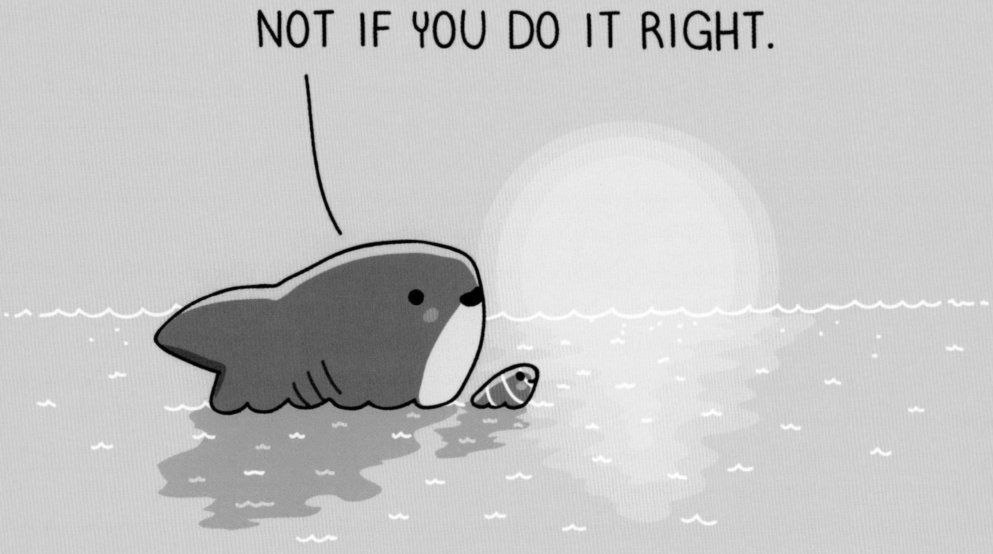
NOT IF YOU DO IT RIGHT.

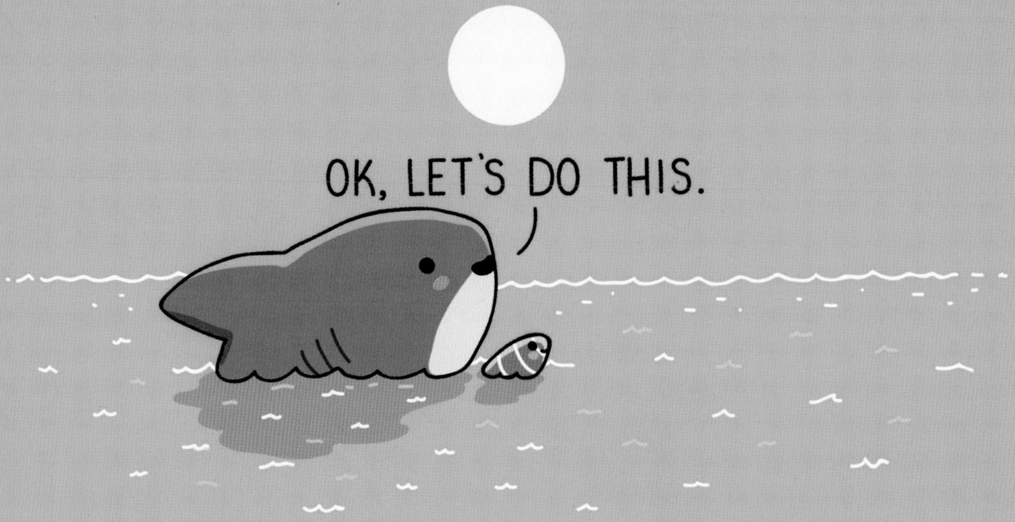
OK, LET'S DO THIS.

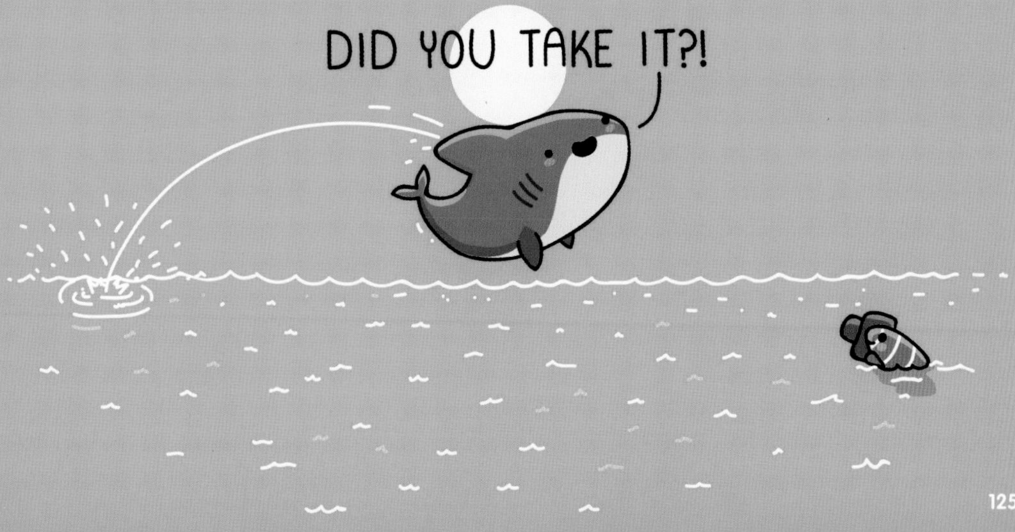
DID YOU TAKE IT?!

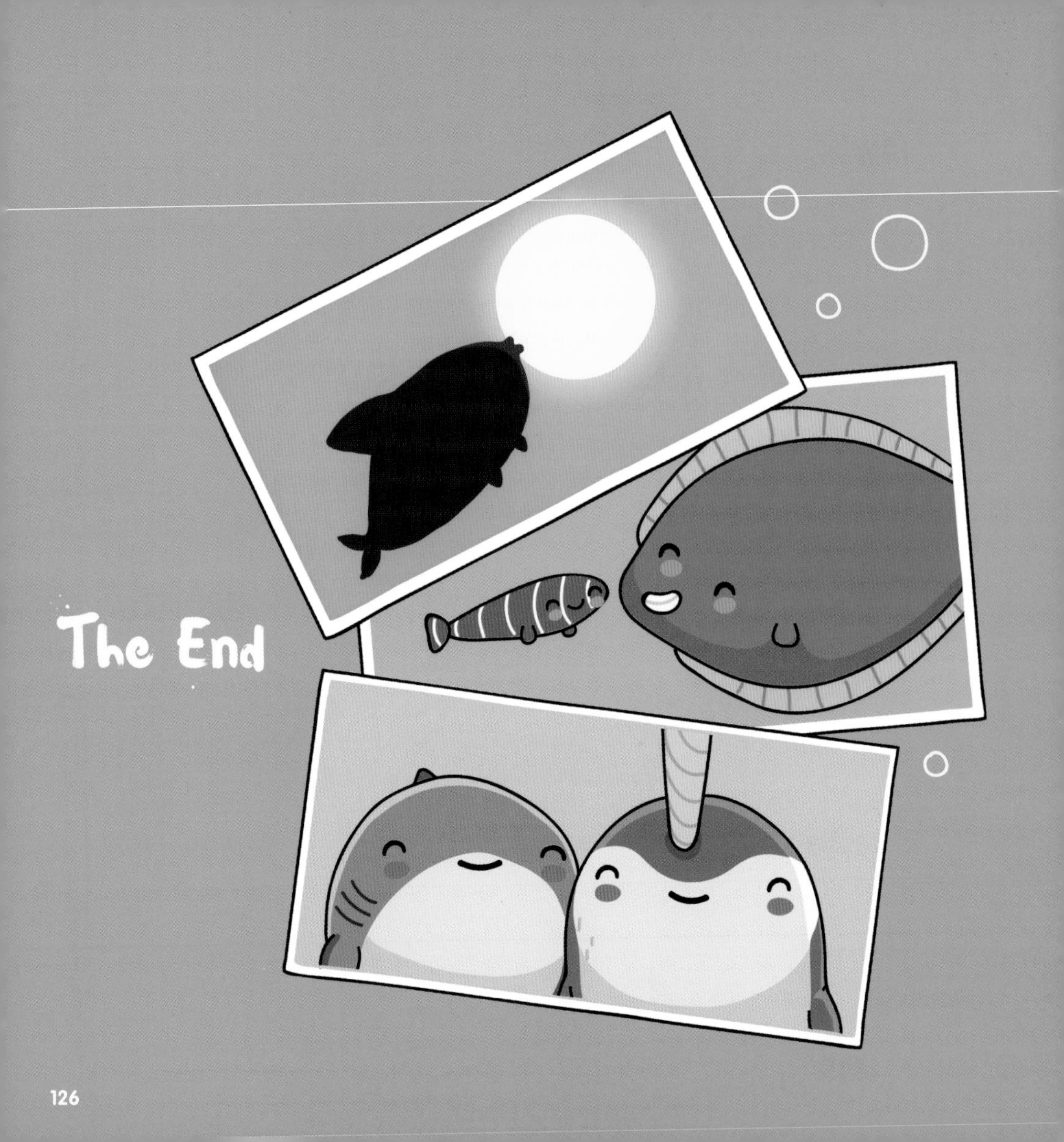

The End

Surprise! This booK has
a soundtracK that will
enhance your experience.

It's available on some of the major
streaming services.

You can find it on
wawawiwacomics.com/wsawK
or by scanning the QR code.

To read more *Wawawiwa* comics,
visit:

@wawawiwacomics

/wawawiwacomics